Carp Fishing

Other titles in the Crowood Fishing Facts series:

River Trout Fishing   Pat O'Reilly
Stillwater Trout Fishing   Chris Ogborne
Fly Tying   Pat O'Reilly
Sea Fishing   Trevor Housby
Pike Fishing   Tony Miles

FISHING FACTS

CARP FISHING

EXPERT ADVICE FOR BEGINNERS

TONY MILES

Illustrations by Stephen Harper

The Crowood Press

First published in 1991 by
The Crowood Press Ltd
Ramsbury, Marlborough
Wiltshire SN8 2HR

British Library Cataloguing in Publication Data

Miles, Tony *1944–*
Carp fishing: expert advice for beginners.
1. Angling
I. Title
799.1752

ISBN 1 85223 474 1

Typeset by PCS Typesetting, Frome, Somerset BA11 1EB
Printed and bound in Great Britain by
BPCC Hazell Books, Aylesbury

Contents

A memorable Cassien monster.

Introduction

Without a doubt, carp are now the most popular coarse fish amongst British anglers, many hundreds fishing for nothing else in both summer and winter. Throughout angling history, there has never been a better chance for the average angler to connect with a big carp than today. This is a legacy of the excitement generated by the upsurge of interest in carp fishing attributed to the exploits of Richard Walker and his friends in the post-war years. That interest led to the deliberate stocking of many waters up and down the country with fast-growing strains of carp, resulting in the abundance of big fish with which we are now blessed. It is interesting to reflect that in the early fifties, one of the conditions of membership of the exclusive Carp Catchers' Club was to provide evidence of having caught a carp of over 10lb in weight. By today's standards, when the capture of 30-pounders is almost a daily event, that is laughable. It does, however, demonstrate the relative scarcity of both carp and carp anglers in those formative years.

Anglers of the nineties wishing to pursue big carp have many waters at their disposal where they can realize their goal. Anyone wishing to fish for 20-pounders can find them, and carp of that size are now so common that a fish has to be over 25lb for it to be out of the ordinary. Above that weight, there is a rapid tailing off in numbers and a 30-pounder is still classed as the fish of a lifetime for the majority of anglers. Having said that, the top waters now contain many fish over 30lb and of these, 40lb is an attainable target. I would, however, like to give one word of warning to younger anglers coming into carp angling. With no other species is there such a danger of setting your sights far too high initially, by reading the exploits of others in the weekly publications. Remember, those men are at the very pinnacle of carp angling. Even with the quality of carp fishing available today, a 10-pounder is still a good fish, a 20-pounder a specimen, and a 'thirty' truly exceptional.

Another reason for the upsurge in catches of very big carp since the war is the large number of flooded gravel pits that have resulted from the increased demand for building materials. Gravel pits provide the conditions for all species of fish to attain large weights and carp are certainly no exception.

Carp are to be found in all types of water throughout the country, from estate lakes and gravel pits to canals and rivers. Big

INTRODUCTION ————————————————

fish are to be found in all these, but there is no doubt that the really exceptional heavyweights come from large pits.

In the last few years pioneering carp anglers who yearn for even bigger specimens have turned their attentions to the fishing that is available overseas (particularly in France, Holland and Spain) and as a result some truly awe-inspiring carp have been landed. The opening of the Channel Tunnel will make fishing in France easily accessible to all who wish to avail themselves of it, and there are some exciting possibilities ahead. Personally, I have only experienced one carp fishing trip abroad which probably spoiled me a little as, after a near disastrous start, it turned out to be really memorable.

Andy Barker and I shared ten days on the shores of Lake Cassien in the south of France in April 1986, and for the first six days we were forced to endure almost uninterrupted torrential rain. During that period, there was not the slightest sign of a fish, the lake rose an incredible 3ft, and the whole trip was turning into a depressing nightmare. On the seventh day, however, the weather started to change for the better, and at the first hint of sunshine the carp began to move at last. That first evening we each landed one fish: a 32-pounder to me and a 26-pounder to Andy. That well-deserved initial success was but the aperitif for my main course, which was to be served at lunchtime the following day.

I had a very slow run, and at first I put this down to bream, which had been a bit of a nuisance. As I struck, however, I quickly realized the error of my diagnosis as the rod was nearly ripped from my hands and a huge fish powered away, heading for a boulder-strewn far bank, about a 100yd distant. As the fish headed for certain disaster on those rocks, I increased the pressure in an attempt to turn it, and it took all the strength at my command to keep the rod up. The 18lb Sylcast line made a high-pitched whining sound as the carp eventually stopped, only about 5yd short of its objective. There was then a sight I have relived in my mind's eye a hundred times. A gigantic fish completely left the water and turned over before heading off at speed to my left. Even at a 100yd range, I knew it was gigantic.

After that initial run, I was never really in serious trouble again, although my heart stayed in my mouth until Andy finally closed the net mesh around it. For a long time we were both speechless as we gazed at a leviathan amongst carp. The weight we recorded was 58lb exactly, a fish far beyond my wildest dreams.

When I am asked what is the most memorable fish of my angling career, there is simply no contest. That French monster occupies this exalted position.

Particle feeding.

CARP LOCATION _____

Some of our largest carp are to be found in the multitude of gravel pits that exist in this country, and which are being created steadily because of the increasing demands for road-building materials. Gravel pits can vary from picturesque little fisheries, surrounded by woodland and containing lush weed growth, to huge, inhospitable and barren waterscapes. Obviously, the more mature the pit, the more nature will have attempted to heal all the man-made scars, but it does not follow that the most mature pits contain the biggest carp. In fact, sometimes quite the reverse is true. Therefore, when assessing the potential of a gravel pit it is a matter of observation and of gleaning as much information from other anglers and press reports as possible.

Visual Location

The most reliable method of locating carp is either to actually see them for yourself or to observe evidence of their presence. Undoubtedly, spotting the fish is usually more difficult than in natural lakes, because of the size and depth of some of the pits, and because the banks are often exposed, making the surface of the water susceptible to the slightest breeze and producing varying amounts of ripple.

The most obvious method of visual location is to see the carp jump or roll on the surface, and I would strongly recommend that you invest in a powerful pair of binoculars. Regularly using them to scan the water can yield a great deal of useful information that could otherwise take a long time to gather. As well as the very obvious leaping and noisy rolling, carp also have a habit of breaking the water quite silently, so that perhaps half of the body is temporarily visible. Such porpoise-like behaviour can be repeated two or three times in quick succession. This is useful as not only does it locate the fish but it also indicates the direction in which it is moving.

On those days when the carp are not showing themselves, methods of visual location can include observing localized colouring of the water (although this is quite rare on gravel pits), vortices caused by carp swirling below the surface, and movements of weedbeds as fish pass through them. I would strongly recommend that you keep a dossier of every water you fish, religiously noting down all your observations on each trip. In that way, it should not be too long before you are able to draw some positive conclusions.

If you use binoculars to look for evidence of carp, even the strongest wind may not be a detriment to their observation. Wind certainly stimulates gravel pit carp into activity, and they roll regularly in rough conditions. A carp roll in choppy water is very characteristic as a pronounced flat spot is created in the waves for a few seconds. The wind in fact is a very useful ally in the location of gravel pit carp since, even when the fish are not showing themselves, the carp will usually migrate to the windward end of the pit. The stronger the wind and the longer it has been sustained in a particular direction, the more true this statement will be.

Obvious physical features in a pit are always worth investigating, such as weedbeds, beds of lilies, areas of snags, overhanging trees, and so on. Particularly reliable are gravel islands out in the main body of the pit, especially if they are adorned by overhanging foliage. On many waters, the margins of such islands are often

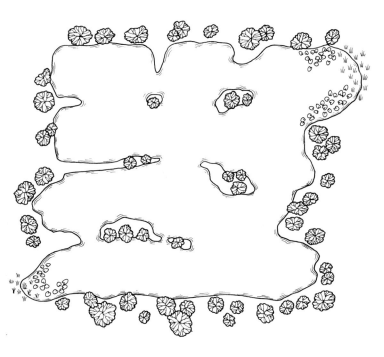

A typical gravel pit.

CARP LOCATION

'Such porpoise-like behaviour . . .'

the most reliable areas of the lot, as the carp spend much of their time browsing around them.

As a general rule, the larger the pit and the lower the stock density of carp, the more difficult their location by visual means alone. Then we have to rely on a combination of experience, common sense and watercraft to find them. It is essential to familiarize yourself thoroughly with as much of the bottom contours of the water as possible. There are several ways in which this can be achieved.

Mapping a Water

Obviously, if you are permitted to use a boat mapping the water will be possible in a fraction of the time it would take from the bank. From a boat, it is certainly easier if the task is undertaken on a bright, windless day. The sun will allow you to see the shallower gravel bars as well as weedbeds, sunken snags and so on. The lack of wind allows accurate mapping without the annoyance of

12

excessive drift. For areas where the depth is too great to see the bottom, the use of a long-handled pole marked in 1ft divisions is recommended. The best pole to equip yourself with is the type used to clean out swimming pools and which can be extended to about 16ft. As an extra refinement, a garden leaf rake-head can be adapted to fit one end of the pole. With this, not only can the depth be found, but the bottom composition as well.

As you drift slowly around the water, you can gradually draw up a picture of where the gravel bars are, where the bottom consists of gravel, mud or silt, where the weed is sparse and where it is thick, and so on. Once you have found the extent and direction of the gravel bars, you have located important features for the location of carp. In all pits these bars are used as highways by the fish at one time or another, and the gullies between them often attract the formation of silt beds, which encourage the breeding of bloodworms. The base of a bar often has a particularly large silt accumulation, and a carp bait arranged to fish in that position has a good chance of being accepted.

Obviously, when mapping from a boat, the fastest method of all is to use an echo-sounder. There are several excellent models on the market, all very simple to use. If you have access to a sounder you will save yourself hours of laborious work.

If you cannot use a boat then you have no choice but the long-winded method of searching from the bank with sliding floats. It takes a tremendously long time to familiarize yourself with even a fraction of a large pit in this manner, and you are limited to the maximum casting range. Nevertheless, many carp have been landed after features have been located by this method. The technique I use is to cast out a large, easily visible float and large lead as far as possible, initially with a shallow depth setting. Gradually ease it back towards you, and if the float pops above the water at any part of the retrieve you have found an area shallower than the set depth. If this procedure is repeated at progressively deeper settings, eventually you will have a detailed picture of the features immediately in front of you. By working the same way systematically 50yd to the left and right, you will eventually have a rough idea of the bottom geography to maximum casting range over 100yd of bank. Areas located by such an exercise will at least give you a clue as to where to place your hookbaits, and will allow you to fish with much more confidence.

CARP LOCATION ────────────────

Estate lakes are those waters that have either been artificially created by damming small streams or which occur naturally as the 'farm pond' type of water. Shallow water supply reservoirs, which are also formed by damming shallow valleys, are also included in this category.

The main feature of a typical estate lake and which differentiates it from a gravel pit, is that it will be very much shallower on average, with more weed growth and often heavily-tree-lined banks.

The bottom composition will be totally different, consisting either of deep mud, silt or clay. As many estate lakes have been landscaped in such a way as to be totally surrounded by trees, the bottom of such a water will often contain the remains of many years of rotting leaves. This has the effect of creating a deep layer of bottom sediment.

Visual Location

Location of carp in such waters is a much simpler matter than in large gravel pits. The fish are more prone to showing themselves, or at least betraying their whereabouts by other unmistakable signs. As with all carp, they delight in rolling and crashing on the surface, or head-and-tailing like porpoises. In shallow lakes, even when they are not showing themselves as such, they often swim so close to the surface that slight ripples and bow waves allow us to locate them. This bow waving is very useful as a carp will often move a long way in this manner, thus telling us the direction in which it is swimming.

Another common phenomenon that you may see is a very shallow, faint V shape cutting through the water, and if you use your binoculars you will often see that this is caused by a carp swimming with just the extreme tip of its dorsal fin breaking the surface. Such cruising fish are usually not feeding, but at least you know where they are.

As with gravel pit carp, estate lake fish have an affinity for weedbeds of all species, and they particularly like those types under which they can bask on a bright day. Surface lilies and beds of the floating plant potamogeton are always worthy of thorough investigation.

Surface feeding in lilies.

Estate lake carp are great margin patrollers, and they particularly like areas of overhanging bushes and trees, or marginal beds of rushes, reedmace or Norfolk reeds. Places where trees overhang the margins, and especially where branches have fallen in to create snags, are particularly favoured by carp as they feel secure in such areas. If you approach such an area carefully, you will often see the swirls of feeding fish as they forage under the roots. Wide beds of marginal plants such as rushes are also very reliable carp-holding areas, and the fish betray their presence very easily when they brush through the stems as they search for food. When you see a path through rushes you have found carp.

In areas where there are no obvious physical features, one of the best ways of locating feeding carp is to look for patches of colouring in the water. This is rare on hard-bottomed gravel pits, but is extremely common on estate lakes. The beauty of locating fish in this way is that not only have you found where they are, but you also know that they are feeding.

15

CARP LOCATION

Rushes are reliable holding areas.

An extension to the coloured water method of carp location is to find one individual large fish that is moving leisurely through the bottom silt, feeding as it goes. This produces a classic path of coloured water, and such a carp is known as a 'smoke screener' for obvious reasons.

Another reliable method of finding carp is to watch for the distinctive bubbling as they feed. When the fish have their snouts stuck in the lake bottom, rooting around for whatever food is present, they send clouds of bubbles to the surface as entrapped gases are filtered through their gills. Again, bubblers are feeding fish, although they may be feeding in a very preoccupied manner.

Bottom Topography

Generally speaking, estate lakes do not have the great variance of bottom contours so common in gravel pits, so that even on those days when the fish are not showing themselves, you can make an accurate assessment of where they are likely to be. Any area con-

16

taining an obvious feature such as a weedbed or snag, a small area of hard bottom of either gravel or rock, or perhaps a depression in the lake bottom, will at some time be colonized by carp. The same goes for any marginal area which is sheltered. However, the margins under large deciduous trees can be unproductive after the autumn, as the falling leaves can quickly deoxygenate and sour the water.

Perhaps the most obvious method of location, especially on some of the more heavily fished waters, is to fish those areas which get a lot of attention from other anglers and where, therefore, large quantities of bait are regularly introduced. Carp are very adept at taking advantage of such an easy food supply and while it is true to say that the fish may progressively become more difficult to tempt on a hookbait, at least you know where they are.

Influence of Wind

The biggest difference between the carp of estate lakes and those of gravel pits in my experience is that the lake fish seem much less influenced by the wind. There are exceptions to this, Redmire being the most famous, but on all the lakes I fish, the location of the fish appears to be totally independent of wind direction. This could be because the nature of lakes often means they are a lot more sheltered than their pit counterparts. Also, because they are generally shallower and have more even bottom contours, there are not the same underwater currents created by a strong wind. Also, true estate lakes rarely cover more than a few acres. If you fish a very large lake or extensive shallow reservoir, the wind direction could be a more critical factor. You will only find this out at any particular water by observation, and trial and error.

The carp of shallow lakes are very responsive to surface baits, and another good location method is to drift free offerings such as chum mixers down wind. It may take some time to stir interest in the carp, but eventually you should find them starting to feed. As well as being a very effective ploy in finding some fish, it is also very exciting.

17

CARP LOCATION _____

There are undoubtedly huge carp in stretches of some rivers and canals, but as they are almost invariably localized, the first essential in the location of these fish is a little local knowledge as to where to start. Once you know that you are in the correct general area, then you can begin looking for the fish in specific swims. Without that local knowledge, you could waste an awful lot of valuable time in fruitless searching.

Much of what has already been written about location techniques in stillwater will apply to the carp of rivers and canals. They will still display the same affinity for weedbeds, islands, depressions in the river bed and underwater snags. In rivers, they are particularly attracted to overhanging marginal vegetation, and the classic type of raft chub swim is one which any carp will colonize eagerly. The small head of resident carp in the Cherwell, a river I know well, are almost invariably found in swims of this type, alongside the chub.

Visual Location

Many rivers and streams containing carp are certainly clear and shallow enough in the summer months for visual location to be a viable proposition. Where they are present, they are very obliging fish, showing themselves readily, and a few hours spent walking the banks on a summer day could reap handsome rewards.

It is a mistake to imagine that river carp will always be found in sluggish or still water. They are quite capable of thriving in fast flows, but are happiest in areas of smooth, steady currents. Runs of smooth water just off the main flow, steady water under a high bank, and where the water deepens and slows downstream of shallows will all contain carp, if any are present at all.

There have been an amazingly large number of good carp taken from weir pools, generally in the return flows along the margins or in the weir run-out, and small side-streams are also worth investigating. Obviously, if your river contains carp and you know of a warm-water outfall, that will almost certainly be a hot spot in more ways than one.

The best carp in canals seem to thrive where the canal is most neglected and where the marginal plants have been given a chance to establish themselves. Some of the better spots are where

Rivers and Canals

the canal widens out into a basin and there are wide rush bed margins. Naturally, any area where there are water lilies will attract the fish, as will overhanging trees. Very rarely will a tow-path bank have the necessary cover, and when canal carp fishing it is almost invariably more productive to present baits under the opposite margins. Carp will be attracted to marginal irises, rushes, reedmace and lilies. The denser the foliage, the more likely the carp are to colonize the area, and if a canal is totally unused so that stretches are completely clogged with weed, then that could be a very reliable area indeed.

Perhaps one of the most consistent spots to locate canal carp is adjacent to lock cuttings, and some of the biggest carp from Midland canals have been taken from such areas.

Carp love overhanging foliage.

TACKLE AND TECHNIQUES _____

There are so many excellent rods and reels on the market nowadays that it is largely a matter of personal preference which you select.

Rods

Rods, however, should exhibit differing characteristics for the various kinds of carp fishing that might be undertaken. An ideal rod for presenting a lobworm to a margin-feeding bubbler may manifestly be unsuitable for hurling a heavy lead 100yds. I content myself with two sets of carp rods, a $2^1/_4$lb test curve, 11ft Tricast for short- to medium-range work and a 12ft, $2^3/_4$lb test Tricast ER for longer range fishing. I select Tricast because the action of the blanks suits me and even the ER version has sufficient feel to enjoy the fight of a big carp in the margins. The main drawback with many long-range carp rods in my opinion, is that they are too steeply tapered for the fight from a carp to be enjoyable. Also, a very unforgiving fast-tapered blank can give problems with hooks pulling out of a fish at short range, if the carp gives sudden lunges.

Reel

The choice of reel will depend largely on whether you fight carp by back winding or by use of the clutch. If you backwind, any good fixed-spool reel will suffice provided that the line lay is good enough to allow long casts and the spools are of adequate capacity. They should be capable of carrying at least 200yd of 12lb line.

If you play carp off a clutch, as I do, then the reel you select must have a reliable drag mechanism. An unreliable and variable clutch is worse than useless. For several years I used my ABU 755 Cardinals without any problem, ABU clutches being superb on all their range of reels. Over this last season, however, I have switched to Shimano Aero GT 4000 baitrunners, which really are terrific tools. Not only do they have extremely sensitive and reliable drag adjustments, stern mounted for ease of manipulation, but the baitrunner facility is one that is a boon for carp anglers generally. It has done away with the necessity for anglers who use a slipping clutch to fish open bales, with the problems that this can sometimes create, especially in windy conditions..

Line

Variations of actual terminal rigs are found on later pages, but the other basic items of line and hooks are of vital importance. The two most popular lines for carp angling are Maxima and Sylcast, and not without good reason. Both are superb lines, immensely strong and of even quality. Of the two, Maxima is slightly more supple and is my usual choice. However, if your fishing is carried out in gravel pits, you may be better advised to plump for Sylcast, as it has better abrasion resistance. Whichever line you use, it should be changed regularly – at least twice a season.

Hooks

The subject of carp hooks is one that could occupy a small book of its own, and I do not intend to get involved in a lengthy discussion on them. All I would say is that I have used Au Lion d'Or

Standard two-rod set-up.

hooks for all my fishing where sizes 2 to 8 are called for, and they have never let me down yet. I have always maintained that the offset bend and inturned point aid efficient hooking because they twist to take a grip at whatever angle they enter the carp's mouth. Strangely enough, the modern bent-hook varieties have been introduced to give just this effect.

Nets and Scales

As far as the ancillary tackle is concerned, the first essential is a good, big landing net, which should have a mesh made of either micromesh or carp sacking material. I would recommend a triangular net with at least 42in arms. Next, you need a soft weighsling, carp sacks and a set of reliable scales capable of weighing fish up to 40lb. If you are fishing some of the top waters these days, even 40lb scales may not be adequate and you may decide to purchase dial scales weighing up to 60lb. I use 40lb Avon scales, but brass Salter scales are just as accurate.

Rod Rests and Bite Indicators

Rod-rest systems and bite indication have undergone quite a revolution in recent years and there are many superb systems available. If you elect to use normal rod rests, equip yourself with sturdy stainless steel ones with adjustable height settings so that you can cope with any uneven banks. You can use either individual rests for each rod or utilize buzzer bars for multiple rod carrying. If you elect single rests with buzzer bar assemblies, fit each rod rest with an anti-twist boot, available from tackle shops, or you will find that the whole lot will tend to swivel in a strong wind or if you knock it. The bite alarm will be fitted on to the front rests or buzzer bar and the most popular are Optonics. These are very reliable audible indicators which have withstood the test of time, but they should be maintained regularly. Do not forget to carry spare batteries in your bag. In very windy conditions, it is sometimes advisable to clip the line into line clips mounted on the rod just in front of the Optonic to prevent constant annoyance from bleeps caused by the line blowing between the sensors of the alarm. Clips positioned thus will obviously prevent drop-back bites from registering, but that is the lesser of two evils in very wild weather.

As well as an audible alarm, it is necessary to have a visual one as well, and most carp anglers employ monkey climbers in conjunction with their Optonics. Be very careful when choosing your climber because many simply seize under tension. It is wise to buy top-quality stainless needles and low-friction monkeys. And make sure you keep them spotlessly clean, or the monkeys will continually stick. I would recommend using fairly heavy monkeys, such that drop-back bites will be efficiently registered, and ones which incorporate a slot into which a betalight can be inserted for night fishing.

Many anglers these days use specially designed rod pod assemblies, which were first introduced to combat the rock-hard banks of gravel pits. In actual fact, they are very good for all carp angling, since once in position the rests and monkey-climb needles cannot move and everything is nice and solid.

Other Tackle

Most long-stay carp anglers use a bivouac, or bivvy, these days, and again it is a matter of personal preference whether you use one or not. For a session of 24 hours or less, I do not bother, contenting myself with sheltering under a 50in umbrella. The problem with a bivvy is that it makes you disinclined to move if you spot fish feeding elsewhere.

If you intend to do much long-stay carping then you have to consider your comfort if you are going to fish efficiently. The first essential is a comfortable bed. You should also invest in a good quality sleeping bag and a reliable stove and lightweight cooking utensils for self-catering on the bank.

The most important item is a large dustbin liner, for taking away all your rubbish at the end of your stay. Many carp anglers, I am afraid, have the often deserved reputation of being irresponsible in the amount of litter they leave behind. Leaving litter is as unnecessary as it is unforgivable. Please, please, take your litter home!

TACKLE AND TECHNIQUES

It is a mistake to think that fishing for carp at night automatically increases the chances of success. I get many more runs in the daylight than ever I do at night. However, there are some big advantages in night fishing. Firstly, you can spend a few days in one swim, thereby giving whatever baiting technique you are using an extensive trial without undue disturbance to the fish by continual comings and goings. Secondly, it is certainly more convenient for the angler to be able to remain in place, rather than waste valuable time packing and unpacking gear, not to mention the expense of travelling backwards and forwards.

However, there are circumstances where fishing at night increases the chances of catching carp. Your particular water may be available to other watersport enthusiasts during the day, and if this involves the use of power boats, I for one find it impossible to fish seriously. Also, a good general fishery may be crowded during the day. On waters of this type, the bankside disturbance can drive the carp a long way offshore, but they will move in to the margins during the dark hours to feed.

Equipment

If you are embarking on your first night session, it is vital to go properly equipped or it may well be a cold, wet and miserable affair. Always take plenty of clothing. Even in summer, the night can be surprisingly chilly, and I have worn a thermal suit more than once in June. These days, I wear army surplus jumpers and trousers for my fishing, and always have my thermal suit available, just in case. Waterproof top clothing is a must for wet weather, and I have always worn a wax jacket. As an extra precaution for very wet conditions, a lightweight waterproof jacket and overtrousers are kept in my bag. A pair of long thermal socks and good boots completes the kit.

For fishing at night, a warm sleeping bag will ensure extra comfort, but I never zip it up. I want to be on my feet in seconds if a run develops, and if the alarm goes off when I am fast asleep, the last thing I want to be doing is fumbling with a zip in the dark. I therefore leave my bag totally unzipped and just throw it over me.

Night Fishing

Preparation

An exciting sight – big carp rolling in the moonlight.

Everything you are likely to need should be kept tidy and close to hand, so that you make minimum use of a torch. Although you should have a torch with you for safety reasons and for rebaiting and unhooking fish, try to get into the habit of using it as little as possible. Irresponsible anglers have lost many night fishing concessions, and torches flashing around in the small hours will not impress landowners. The same goes for noise. Even normal conversation carries a long way over water at night, so please refrain from shouting and swearing. It is not funny, and can lead to fishing bans.

Before you ever contemplate a night sortie to a water, make sure that you are thoroughly acquainted with it in daylight. Midnight is not the ideal time to find out that there is an unexpected snag in front of you, or that where you thought it was safe for wading there is 3ft of quicksand. Be aware of your safety, and with this in mind make a point of spending your first few night trips with a friend. It is surprising how many strange sounds you will hear and eerie shadows you will see. With two of you, these natural phenomena can be laughed off for what they are, but on your own, your imagination can take over and leave you badly unnerved.

TACKLE AND TECHNIQUES ─────────

One of the most exciting methods of carp fishing is stalking individual fish. The method is mobile and calls for the minimum of gear: just rod, landing net and a small rucksack will suffice.

Bubblers

The first fish that respond to stalking are the bubblers, those carp that send up clouds of bubbles as they forage in the lake bed. As these fish are often preoccupied with natural food such as bloodworms, they can be frustratingly difficult to tempt, and the most successful method will usually be to try a natural bait for them. There is no better bait for a bubbler than a large lobworm, or a bunch of redworms or maggots. Inject a little air in their tails to give the bait a slow sinking natural appearance.

No better bait for a bubbler than a lobworm.

26

Stalking Carp

Although I am always happiest when using a natural bait for bubblers, they will take things such as pastes or boilies, provided that the bait presentation is not alarming. The most obvious method would appear to be free-lining, but in practice I do not favour this one for two reasons. Bubblers and smoke-screeners feed hard in a small area, and free-lining carries the real risk of foul hooking. Also, the bite indication is not positive enough for my liking. It is too easy for a carp to be deeply hooked before a bite is seen. If possible, I like to use a small self-cocking float or, failing that, a bolt rig with the line hard on the bottom. This arrangement prevents the carp swallowing the bait on the spot. It will have felt the lead and bolted before, giving an obvious bite.

Stalking amongst Foliage

The most exciting method of stalking is using surface baits for carp that are seen feeding among or at the edge of thick foliage. If a carp is spotted moving through lily pads or rushes, a carefully positioned piece of breadcrust, floater, or particles such as chum mixers will be the most effective ploy.

For fishing amongst lily pads, I like to place the hookbait so that it is resting hard against one of the pads, with the line lying over them. In this way, the line is invisible to the carp and the presentation is as natural as you can possibly make it. Also, because the line is all out of the water, it can be as strong as you deem necessary. Do not use weak tackle for such fishing. There is no way you can play a carp as such in a jungle of weeds. It will be a case of hook, hold and haul, and you need tackle strong enough to cope with such tactics.

If you find that a bubbling carp refuses to take a hookbait, it is well worth trying promoting a little preoccupied feeding of your own. By introducing a dozen or so bait droppers of hempseed or other small particles in a confined area and arranging a bait to sit in the middle, you will often take a carp or two quite quickly when they move back into the area.

There is nothing in the rules that confines stalking carp to the daylight hours. Careful creeping round the lake margins at night will often reveal swirls of feeding fish right in the margins. A carefully introduced bait will often meet with an immediate response.

TACKLE AND TECHNIQUES ─────────────

Many waters these days simply have too much pressure on them most of the time for stalking the carp to be viable, and the fishing has to be more static. In carp angling's early days, the basic method was simple free-lining with large baits such as a ball of bread paste, and that method caught plenty of fish. Our modern carp, however, are altogether more sought after and more educated than their brethren of yesteryear, and slightly more sophisticated methods are required to catch them.

The inherent weaknesses with free-lining are, firstly, that you are limited to the casting range dictated by the size of the bait. Even with a large ball of paste, that is not going to be very far. Secondly, with yards of slack line out, bite detection is a bit hit and miss; the bait could be moved several yards before anything was seen at the rod, especially if the fish was running towards you at night. This can lead to many bites being missed, carp being deeply hooked and occasional hooks being bitten off by the carps pharyngeal teeth.

Simple Ledgering

The first development from basic free-lining was straightforward ledgering, which allows a much earlier indication of a bite, the principle being that the shorter the hook link, the sooner the bite indication would be noticed.

The simplest ledgering rig, and one on which I took a great number of carp in the sixties, is one in which an Arlesey bomb is mounted free running directly on the main line, being stopped by a bead and swivel to which the hook link is attached. Because the bomb is directly on the line, this rig is really confined to waters with hard, clean bottoms.

Where there is a layer of silt or silkweed on the bottom, it is far better to fish the lead on a separate link connected to a swivel. If the bottom debris is at all tough or there are snags, the lead link can also be of much lower breaking strain than the main line, so that it will break away if the tackle becomes caught up on something. This is called a rotten bottom. This rig will also show its worth if a hooked carp runs through a weedbed. The bomb always attracts weed around it, and if it is being fished directly on the line it can lead to a lost fish, as I know to my cost. Therefore,

28

Standard Ledgering Tactics

In waters where there is no bottom debris but there are substantial weedbeds, it is still a wise precaution to incorporate a rotten bottom in your terminal rig.

Carp taking a simple ledgered paste.

Refined Ledgering

A further refinement to this basic ledgering technique is used when you are fishing over deep weed, where you wish to hold the line on top of the weed rather than allowing it to sink through it. It will minimize snagging on the retrieve or when striking into a fish. The same rotten bottom principle can be employed, but this time you can incorporate a balsa float body on the link. Being buoyant, this will rise to the top of the link and hold the line at that position. Naturally, the link should be as long as the bottom weed is deep. This rig allows us to present a slow sinking bait, say fluffy breadflake, on top of the bottom weed, instead of it being propelled through the weed and possibly being invisible to the fish.

29

When you wish to present a floating bait to carp out of normal casting range, or there is so much wind or drift that a free-lined floater is continually pulled out of position, the answer lies with the anchored floater rig. This is basically a simple derivation of the rotten bottom principle, except that the lead need not be fixed on low strength line unless the bottom is snaggy.

The principle is that a buoyant bait will pull line off the open spool until it reaches the surface, at which the pick-up can be engaged and the slack line taken in. The rig will work with the lead attached to a swivel for very buoyant baits such as a big chunk of crust, but it is far better to substitute the swivel for a large diameter plastic ring, which has next to no friction. With this modification, even small offerings like chum mixers will rise to the surface easily. It is even better if you incorporate in this rig a hook that has been counterbalanced by the addition of a little sliver of cork, superglued to the back of the shank.

To prevent damage to the hook knot, always include in the rig a bead that the plastic ring cannot pass over, and also do not be afraid to use a decent sized lead. The anchored rig works much better with a 2oz bomb than it does with one weighing only $\frac{1}{2}$oz. The heavier the lead, the more positive the bite indication will be.

Link ledger useful for presenting surface bait.

Drawbacks

One of the major drawbacks with fishing on the surface is the attentions of ducks, swans, seagulls and so on. With free-lining floaters, there is very little you can do except strike off your bait if the birds become too persistent. With the anchored rig, you can if you wish, fish with the tackle taut enough so that the hookbait is fished just below the surface. If there is a slight ripple this will certainly disguise the bait long enough for the carp to have first crack

30

Anchored Floating Bait

it. The birds will eventually find it of course, but this little trick will at least allow you to fish in peace for a while.

The deeper the water, the more difficult it becomes to get the anchored rig to fish properly, and the trick is to use the longest bomb link possible, including a balsa float body, so that the bait has the minimum amount of travel. It is obviously impossible to cast a rig including a 12ft bomb link, but you can try coiling the link carefully and tying it with two or three pieces of PVA string. This is then simple to cast, and after a minute or two in the water, the PVA dissolves, allowing the balsa to take the link to its full extension. The only drawback with this is when playing a fish with 12ft of line swinging around with a heavy bomb on the end. For this reason, it is always better to fish this version with a bomb link of low breaking strain line, just in case the lead becomes snagged while playing a fish.

Carp approaches anchored floater.

In waters where carp have been fished for extensively, the fish soon become wary of picking up anglers' baits and those that they do take are treated with utmost suspicion. Full-blooded runs used to occur on standard ledgering rigs, but the more usual form of indication today degenerates into frustrating little twitches. The longer range at which you are forced to fish, the more infuriating this problem becomes. There are two solutions; either attempt to hit the twitchers or adapt the terminal rig somehow to promote more positive indications.

Striking at small twitch bites, while it will convert a percentage to carp on the bank, is a very inefficient method of carp angling and is not very relaxing. It is certainly not a method that is viable for the long-stay angler. Another drawback is that continual striking at small indications and recasting with heavy leads combine to make the fish even more nervous, further exacerbating the situation.

Method

The better answer is to adapt the rig into one that encourages the carp to run with the bait. It stands to reason that if a carp feels a sudden resistance when twitching a bait its first reaction will be to bolt in alarm, dropping the bait like a hot potato. However, if the act of picking up the bait and feeling the resistance occur at one and the same time, the carp will often bolt with the bait still in its mouth, which it will then find difficult to eject while travelling fast.

In practice, this can be achieved by fishing with a heavy lead and a very short hook link, and the more resistance is introduced

Semi-fixed bolt rig.

nto the rig, the more dramatic the runs become. The 'standard' bolt rig would utilize a running lead and a hook link of about 6in, but when the fish start to wise up to that, increasing the weight of the lead, making it fixed rather than running, and shortening the hook link to an inch or two all help in prolonging the useful life of the rig.

As an extra refinement, if baits used with the bolt rig variants are arranged on the hook so that the hook point is well exposed, the carp will tend to hook themselves against the resistance of the lead when they bolt.

When using any fixed lead rig, please ensure that it is one where the lead will pull off the line easily in the event of the line breaking above the lead while playing a carp. The fish will shift an unweighted hook soon enough, but if it is dragging a heavy lead around, it could become stuck fast in weeds or tree roots and starve to death. The drawing illustrates a safe way of using fixed leads, which are known as 'semi-fixed' for obvious reasons.

Carp will find bait difficult to eject.

Eventually, even bolt rigs result in twitchy bites, or no bites at all as the carp learn to associate them with danger. What appears to happen is that the carp become so nervous that they learn to move the baits very gently in their lips for an inch at a time as though expecting something to happen. If a resistance is felt, they know that dashing off often leads to a nasty experience, and so they drop the bait on the spot. Carp learn very fast! If they feel nothing, however, they may continue twitching for some time resulting in exactly the same problem as we had with the standard ledgering rigs.

The way round this is to allow the fish to twitch the bait for a few inches without anything untoward occurring, which will hopefully allay its suspicions. If, once confident enough to take the bait properly and move off with it, the carp suddenly encounters a resistance it will tend to bolt with the bait in its mouth.

Semi-fixed shock rig.

Method

The terminal rig to achieve this effect is one in which a short hook link is again employed in conjunction with a heavy lead, but the lead is free to slide to a back stop. If the lead is heavy enough not to be moved by gentle twitching, the carp will take several inches of line through the swivel quite freely, until the back stop jams against the lead, when there is a sudden huge increase in resistance.

Again, it is only experience on any day that determines exactly what dimensions are required for the rig and the hook link length can be varied, as can the distance to the back stop, until the correct combination is found. Obviously, this can only be taken so far, because if the distance to the back stop is too great, there is little point using one and we are back to the problem of constant twitching.

Shock Rigs

As with bolt rigs, care should be taken to ensure that a break above the back stop does not condemn a carp to towing a lead. Under no circumstances should the lead be arranged to slide between two swivels. That is very dangerous. It is far better to have the lead 'semi-fixed' again, by using a bead and sliding stop knot as the back stop. As well as being much safer, it is also adjusted far more easily.

Striking fast carp run.

35

Tackle and Techniques ─────────

These days, when most carp waters are under constant pressure, all the orthodox variations of bolt and shock rigs have long since been discovered by the majority of the fish. They have learned to pick up all baits gently in their lips without moving, and feel for hook or line. Anything dangerous can be discarded, and the angler is totally unaware that a carp has investigated the bait.

The problem of the carp feeling the exposed hook can simply be overcome by burying the hook in the bait, but that renders hooking uncertain except with the softest baits. The major problem, however, is the one of the carp feeling the line, and this is the one that has to be overcome if we are to catch these very shrewd fish.

Method

The answer to the problem lies with the hair rig, where the bait is not mounted on a hook at all, but presented on a fine or soft hair attached to the hook. The theory is simplicity itself. When a carp picks up the bait, provided the hair is of the correct length, the bait appears unfettered and is therefore taken confidently. As the bait goes to the back of the mouth to be crushed by the pharyngeal teeth, the hook naturally follows. At this point, the carp realizes that something is wrong and attempts to eject the hook and bait. The usual result is that the hook lodges in the mouth, pricking the fish and causing it to bolt in alarm. Feeling the resistance of the lead only serves to increase the speed of the bolt, and the carp often hooks itself.

There are several ways of attaching a hair to a hook, as shown in the diagrams, but I prefer the version in which the hair comes off the hook shank about half-way along, held in place by a short length of low-diameter silicon tubing.

The length of hair to use will again depend on how your particular carp respond, but I have found that ³/₄in is generally about right.

Baits and Materials

The reason for using a hair rig in the first place is to encourage the

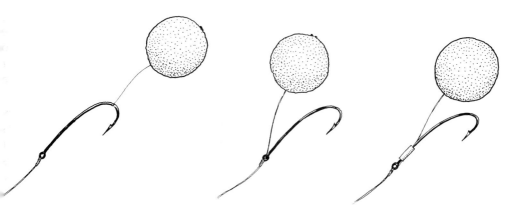

Hair rig variations.

arp to pick up the bait without suspicion and without instantly ejecting it. It therefore follows that the hair material should be as soft and supple as possible, like natural, soft weed. The alternatives we can try are very fine nylon, dental floss, Dacron, Kryston, Gamabraid (Kryston wrapped with Dacron) or Silkworm/Microply (Kryston wrapped with silk). All those materials are extremely limp.

The theory of the hair rig depends on the bait being passed back to the throat teeth for crushing, and it therefore follows that a very soft bait, which could be crushed by the lips, is not ideal for this presentation. Hair rigs are therefore best used in conjunction with hard baits, as this ensures that the hook is well inside the carp's mouth. At this stage, the carp's lips will obviously come into contact with the main line, and this could cause premature rejection. For the hair rig to be at its most effective, therefore, it is best employed with a soft hook link as well as soft hair. Hook link materials available are exactly as mentioned earlier, with the exception of fine nylon of course.

It has become standard practice, whatever your favourite hook link material, to continue that material through the hook eye to form the hair. Initially, it looks wrong because it appears too thick, but it must be remembered that it is the suppleness not the thickness that is important. Think about this. Which would you spit out first, a very thin, sharp fish bone, or a piece of thick but soft cabbage stalk?

Having established that the hair rig works best with hard baits, it

37

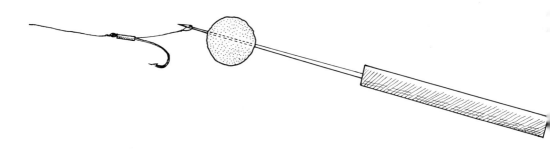

Use of hair rig needle.

stands to reason that modern boiled baits and hard particles are ideal. The best way of attaching baits to a hair is shown in the diagram. Purpose-designed hair rig needles are available commercially, as are special stops to hold the bait on the hair loop once in place. Personally, I find the stops too small and fiddly, especially in wet weather or in the dark, and I prefer to use a long, thin sliver of plastic drinking straw. This is much easier to handle, and once the hair loop has been drawn in place within the body of the bait, the excess plastic can be trimmed off.

One of the major drawbacks in using the modern soft hook link materials for hair rigs is that they require very careful knotting both for attaching hooks and swivels. Personally I use a tucked blood knot with two variations. Firstly, the line is passed through the hook or swivel eye twice instead of once, and secondly

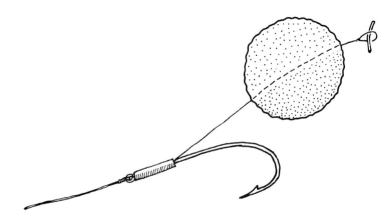

Boilie fixed on hair.

instead of using one tuck I use three. That knot has never let me down yet, on any of the materials mentioned.

Ready for action.

TACKLE AND TECHNIQUES ⎯⎯⎯⎯⎯

On many carp waters, variations on the bolt rig, using limp hook lengths and hair-mounted baits have become standard tackle. These modern approaches to carp fishing have certainly improved catches but like all innovations they have their drawbacks. With ultra-limp hook link materials, the greatest drawback is the one of tangling on the cast, as the hook length wraps itself around the main line above the lead with the force of the cast. Stiffer monofilament can also do this of course, but it happens far less frequently than with softer materials. The problem is so severe that it can happen on virtually every cast.

The Rig

Obviously, this is an unsatisfactory state of affairs and the answer is to make the terminal arrangement as tangle-proof as possible. To this end a whole generation of anti-tangle rigs have evolved. The rigs all have one thing in common, in that they feature a length of rigid tubing, known appropriately as anti-tangle tubing, which is available from all good tackle shops. We are trying to prevent the hook length from wrapping around the main line above the lead and it is easy to see that if the length of tubing used is longer than the hook link, such tangling is impossible.

Obviously, it is still possible for the hook link to catch round the lead. To minimize this, the lead should have as few sharp protuberances as possible on which the terminal link can foul. For this reason, the version using the in-line zipp lead is my favourite rig, being just about 100 per cent tangle resistant.

Anti-tangle rigs.

Anti-Tangle Rigs

The obvious drawback with that version occurs when the lake bed is anything other than clean and hard. With a heavy lead positioned as it is, it is not suitable for fishing in heavy weed. In these circumstances, there is no alternative but to incorporate a rotten bottom in the arrangement. There will be more of a risk of this alternative tangling on the cast, but only between the hook link and bomb link. Although not desirable, this need not be too severe a problem, as the bomb link, being of low breaking strain, will break away anyway if it becomes hung up.

As I write, there has arrived on the market a special gel that can be applied to limp materials to make them stiff until immersion in water, when they very rapidly revert to normal. The gel is perfectly harmless and, in theory, all rigs could be the anti-tangle variety without the use of rig tubing. I am particularly keen to experiment with it on Kryston. The multitude of fine strands can be held together in a stiff link for casting, but after settling on the lake bed, would separate, giving the perfect bait presentation.

One final tip on the anti-tangle rigs shown is using the rig tube. The fine tubing entraps a quantity of air that is impossible to eliminate, and you will find that there is a tendency for the upper part of the tubing to stand clear of the bottom. This is undesirable since it could lead to line bites, and I cure the problem simply by including a lightly pinched AAA shot a few inches above the tube.

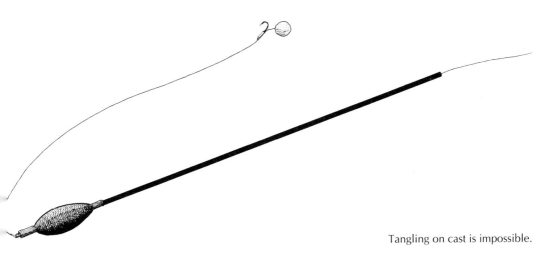

Tangling on cast is impossible.

41

In common with all carp rigs, the fish eventually learn to associate the hair rig with danger, and it is then a case of adopting further modifications to your approach to allay their suspicions. Once they have been caught on hair rigs a few times, they will pick up baits very carefully indeed on the extreme edge of their lips, even though the baits are not actually on a hook. If a fish has been caught several times, say on a rig incorporating a ³/₄in hair, it may have learned to suck a bait for a couple of inches before taking it properly, just to make sure that it is safe. A bait fixed to a hair will obviously not travel as easily as the free offerings and therefore will be rejected.

One way to fool the carp into thinking that the bait on the hair is unfettered is to mount it on an adjustable hair rig, one that will travel some distance unhindered before tightening, at which time the carp will have taken the bait properly.

Method

The two rigs I use for this purpose are the sliding hair rig, and an arrangement known as the 'D' rig. With the sliding version, a small loop is tied into the end of a hair, as shown in the diagram.

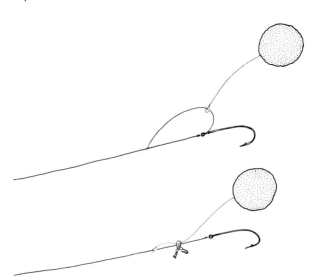

Sliding hair rig variants.

Sliding Hair Rigs

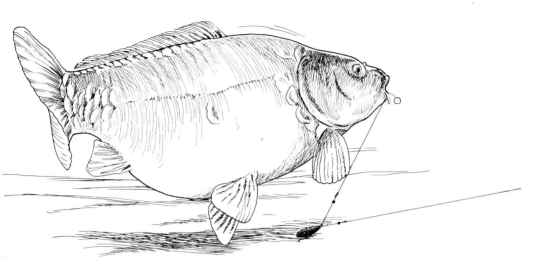

and then fixed in position with a tie of PVA string. As can be seen from the diagram, the loop can be tied as far up the main line as you like, within reason. Personally, I consider about 2in the maximum for practical fishing. The theory is simple enough. Once the rig has been cast out, the PVA dissolves, leaving the loop free to slide. When a nervous carp begins to suck at the bait, it moves quite easily for a couple of inches before the loop catches on the hook bend, creating a sudden increase in resistance. By that time, the carp's suspicions have hopefully been overcome and the bait is well in its mouth, to be followed by the hook.

In the 'D' rig, the principle is very similar, in that the hair loop is free to slide along a D-shaped loop of line tied into the terminal rig as shown. The greater the length of line used to create the 'D' the greater the amount of free travel the bait has. Again, there are practical limits to this, and I do not like the 'D' to stand more than about 2in clear of the hook link. The 'D' rig does not need to be held in place with PVA.

The only drawback with adjustable hair rigs is if the carp runs towards the angler, attempting to take the hair back up the main line. This could lead to missed runs and an increased risk of foul hooking in theory, although this has not happened to me yet in practice.

A big carp is fooled by a sliding hair.

43

TACKLE AND TECHNIQUES _____

A very common feeding trait of carp is a vigorous fanning over the bottom with their powerful fins. This creates vortices which in turn cause disturbance to the lake bed, moving quite large items up to several inches. Anglers' baits are similarly affected and if the hook bait is lying amongst a bed of free offerings the heavy lead will prevent it from responding to the disturbance in the same way the others do. This lack of movement will often be sufficient to deter the carp from taking a bait, especially if it is in a swim that is fished regularly.

Buoyant Baits

The obvious way to overcome this problem is to find some way of making the hook bait act in the same way as do the free offerings. The answer lies in making the bait buoyant or of neutral buoyancy. A buoyant bait is one that floats naturally and therefore can be fished off the bottom at whatever distance is required by the judicious placing of a split shot on the terminal rig. A neutral-buoyancy bait, or semi-buoyant bait as it is sometimes known, is a bait that sinks extremely slowly and comes to rest very lightly on the lake bed. Not only does this type of bait respond very naturally when there are underwater eddies, lifting off bottom very enticingly, but it is also useful when there is a very soft bed. A slow sinking bait is less likely to sink into the bed and become obscured.

Although the best known orthodox buoyant and neutral buoyancy baits are breadcrust, and squeezed and flattened bread-flake respectively, it is with the use of boilies that modern pop-up

Standard pop-up boilie.

Pop-Up Rigs

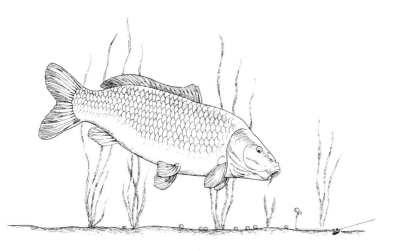

'That looks a tasty morsel.'

carp rigs are principally concerned. Any of the commercially available, frozen-boiled baits can be made to float by baking them for a couple of minutes in the centre of a hot oven or by microwaving them for a few minutes on full power. The exact time is found through trial and error as different baits have different consistencies. I prefer to microwave my baits, and I generally put about thirty in a dish and cover tightly with cling film. They are microwaved for about four minutes and then left to cool for ten minutes or so. At the end of that time, they are then dropped into a tall, clear container of water. There will always be the odd ones that still sink fast, and these are discarded. The rest will be either true floaters or very slow sinkers and these are then separated and put into labelled bait boxes.

The idea of the cling film is to retain as much of the flavour as possible but, whatever you do, baking or microwaving will lead to much of the bait's flavour being lost. This has never seemed to make much difference to my catches but, if it worries you, you can make boilies buoyant by the alternative method of scooping out some of the bait and plugging the hole with sufficient polystyrene to achieve the desired effect. Tackle shops sell small poly balls and buoyant rig foam for this purpose and in the use of pop-up rigs generally. Shop-bought shelf-life boilies are best made buoyant by this method as they do not respond very well to microwaving.

45

TACKLE AND TECHNIQUES

Although I have already mentioned some terminal rigs that are useful in overcoming the problems of bottom weed, bottom debris, or thin layers of silt, all those rigs become extremely cumbersome and unwieldy if a very deep layer of soft bottom weed or liquid mud several feet thick exists. Buoyant or semi-buoyant baits obviously come into their own here, and the most convenient rig to use is the paternoster.

Paternoster rigs can be fished with the hook link either fixed, semi-fixed, or free-running. Quite honestly, when using the paternoster to overcome a soft bottom, it does not make the slightest difference whether you use a free-running or fixed variety. There will be lots of resistance to a biting carp anyway with the bomb sunk in the mud, and I have found that there is no advantage in using one over the other. Whichever you use, always take the precaution of fishing a lighter paternoster link than the main line. In the event of the bomb becoming firmly lodged in bottom debris, it will break away near the lead. This is very important when you have a fish on and could make the difference between landing the carp or losing it. I generally use 12lb Maxima for my carp fishing, but usually incorporate a 6lb bomb link to allow a large margin of safety.

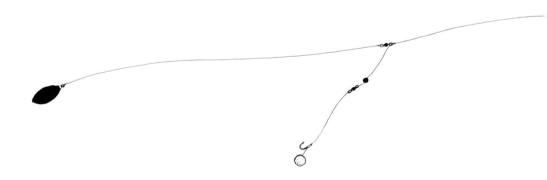

Standard fixed paternoster.

Drawbacks

The greatest drawback to paternoster rigs for carp fishing is when they are used in conjunction with ultra-soft hook link materials. The problem is of tangling on the cast, with the hook link

46

Paternoster Rigs

wrapping itself around the main line. Until very recently, there was little alternative but to revert to stiffer monofilament links for paternoster rigs, but the advent of the new gel for the temporary stiffening of soft materials will revolutionize bait presentation with these rigs. Now, it will be just as effective presenting soft hook links in conjunction with hair-mounted baits as it is with the more widely used bolt rigs already discussed.

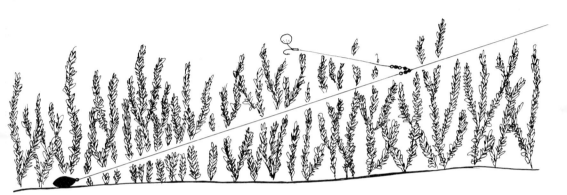

If you are experiencing very tentative bites on paternoster rigs and wish to present a true bolt rig on a very soft lake bottom, then you will have to go to the trouble of manufacturing slow sinking leads which will alight gently on the silt. Obtain a large, drilled bullet lead, cut it in half, and then glue balsa to it until the correct sinking rate is obtained. It is quite fiddly to get the proportion of lead to balsa just right, but is well worth the trouble. One tip: when the finished article is to your satisfaction, give it a good coat of clear varnish before use. That way, you will prevent it becoming waterlogged and useless.

Sliding paternoster for fishing buoyant bait over weeds.

TACKLE AND TECHNIQUES _____

One of the most exciting methods of taking carp is on floating baits. Takes are often spectacular and it can be heart-stopping fishing.

The simplest method of bait presentation is obviously to have nothing on the line at all but hook and bait, and for close-range work, say alongside marginal reeds or lilies, this is the best approach. Even when fishing at close range, a totally unweighted terminal rig is limited by the size of the bait, and the method lends itself to presenting a substantial chunk of breadcrust or large cube of specially prepared high protein floater, both having sufficient casting weight of their own.

Free-Drifting Baits

Totally unfettered baits can also be used at greater range by taking advantage of any offshore breeze, an excellent presentation being to drift free samples steadily down a wind lane, and to follow them with your hook bait. As in most forms of fishing, the longer you spend prebaiting and getting the fish used to your bait, gradually overcoming their natural caution, the greater will be the chances of success when you eventually put a bait on your hook.

When fishing free-drifting baits at range, it is important to maintain close contact with the terminal rig and not allow yards of slack line to billow around. Not only will that make successful hooking uncertain but it will also tend to cause drag on the bait, forming a wake which the carp view with extreme suspicion. For this reason, it is wise also to grease the line to prevent it sinking and creating such drag.

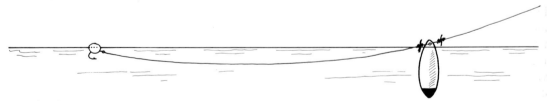

Use of surface controller.

Drifting Floater Fishing

Tackle

For most forms of floater fishing, especially when using light items like buoyant cereals or pet biscuits such as chum mixers, extra casting weight is required to make the tackle manageable. The simplest addition is a small self-cocking float, which not only aids casting but also provides more positive bite detection, especially at range. If I intend to drift a surface particle bait from my own bank down a wind lane, the self-cocking float will be my choice, with plenty of float body visible.

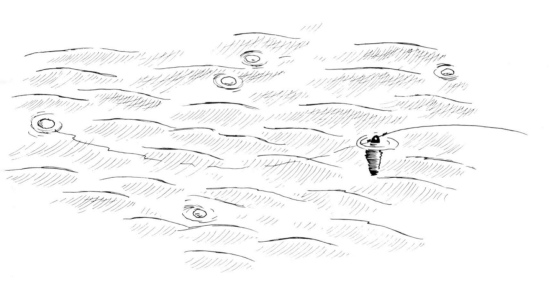

Obviously, the casting range of a float is also limited, and if you have a need to cast a floating bait a long way, say to present a bait alongside rushes 50yd away, then you will need to substitute the float for one of the modern floating carp bombs, which are to all intents and purposes, counterbalanced ledger weights. Equipped with one of those, it is possible to fish efficiently at a similar range as is possible with straightforward ledgering.

Hook bait drifts with free offering.

49

On waters where carp have been hammered on floating baits, they become very wary of them and either ignore them totally or give frustrating little knocks at the bait that are impossible to strike at. Where free offerings are readily accepted but the hook bait is left severely alone, it is almost certainly the line from the float or other controller that is alarming the fish. The way round this problem is to arrange to fish a floating bait with no line touching the water near the hookbait.

Method

The first approach to try is the use of a rig known as the beach-

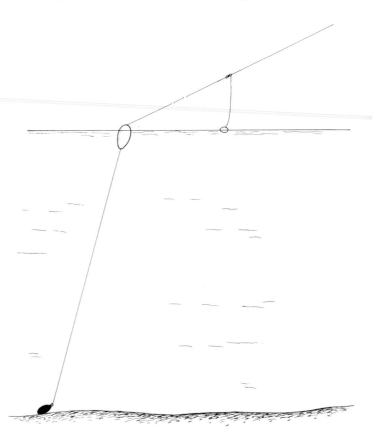

A beachcaster rig.

caster. As can be seen in the diagram, the rig is terminated by a heavy bomb, with a large pike float set above it at the depth of the water. We can see immediately that this limits the effective depth that can be fished with this method. A tail of more than about 8ft would be far too unwieldy to cast far.

The hook length is then set about 2ft or 3ft above the float, the idea being that when the line from rod to float is taut, the hook bait just rests on the water surface. In this way, the bait appears exactly as do the free offerings.

The higher the rod is set on the bank, the better the rig will fish, and special rod rests are now available for this method. Because of the tension in the tackle, takes can be very fierce, wrenching the rod over like the daddy of all barbel bites. It is, therefore, a rig that should not be left to fish for itself. This is an excellent way of losing a rod and more than one angler has seen his or her tackle take off into the water!

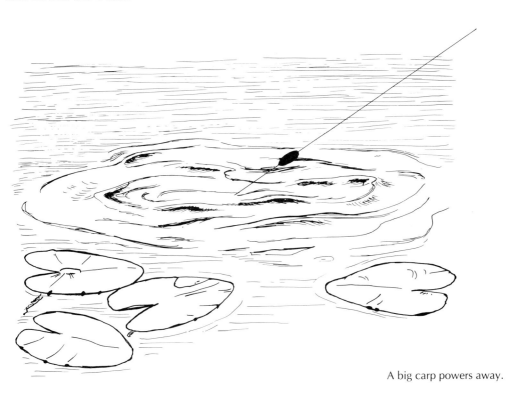

A big carp powers away.

The drawbacks to the beachcaster rig are that it is confined to waters of a depth below about 8ft and because of the way it is set up it is suitable only for presenting a static bait. In the circumstances where you either want to fish an apparently untethered floating bait over deeper water or free drifting, another rig comes into its own, one known as the suspender.

Method

The terminal rig is so simple and yet so ingenious. It consists of a thin, rigid plastic tube, fitted offset with a polyball and counterbalancing weight. It can be seen from the diagram that the angle at which the suspender is fished can be controlled by both the positioning on the tube of the polyball and by the weight of lead used. Ideally, the rig fishes best when the tube is making an angle of no more than 45 degrees to the water surface.

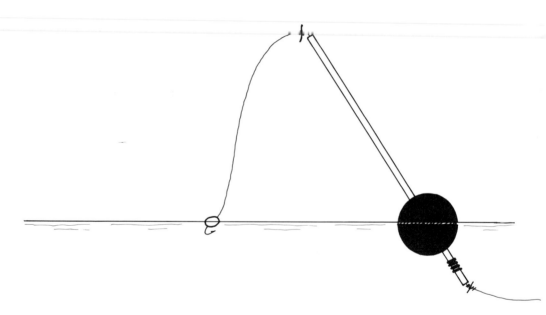

Suspender rig.

It is important to get the hook length exactly right for this method if it is to be at its most effective. Too short, and a very light bait would hang clear of the water, too long and loose line

Suspender Rigs

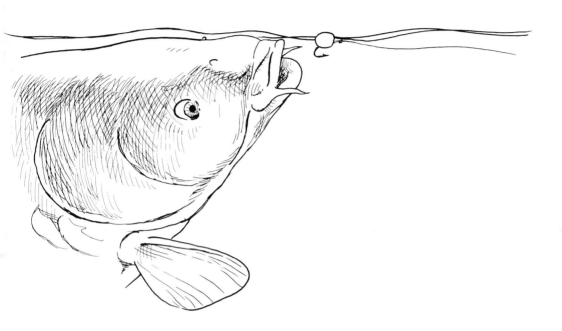

would lie round the hookbait in coils, neither of these being a particularly effective presentation! The best way to make sure that you have it exactly right is to experiment first in the margins, and place ties of power gum at the correct positions above and below the plastic tube to hold it in place.

This carp could be spooked by surface line.

TACKLE AND TECHNIQUES ———————

Andy Barker and I devised a terminal rig for use in overcoming the problems of the snag-ridden bed of Lake Cassien and have labelled it our anti-snagging rig. The problem at Lake Cassien lies in the incredible number of boulders, jagged rocky outcrops and tree stumps that litter the bottom. Not only have we the problem of the terminal rig becoming trapped in such debris, but also the line from bait to rod top as well. A similar situation exists in many English gravel pits where shallow gravel bars lie between you and the bait, especially if the tops of those bars are adorned with razor-sharp zebra mussels, which can cut even the strongest line.

Method

The objective is to hold as much line as possible above the bottom debris, other than the essential short length adjacent to the bait. Even there, the rig is fished incorporating a lead fixed to a rotten bottom. The method is perfectly adaptable to coping with the problem in any depth of water, by adjustment of the sliding stop knot which controls the position of the paternoster float. It can be seen that the line can be arranged to fish as high in the water as you like, within reason. If bottom debris is particularly dangerous, as at Cassien, the line can also be greased from above the float back to the rod.

Cassien anti-snagging rig.

54

Cassien Anti-Snagging Rig

If you do not want to grease the line, it is important to fish the rig quite taut once the bait is in position in order to prevent the line from float to rod from sinking into snags. This rig is therefore best fished in conjunction with heavy monkey climbers fished high on the needles, and butt foam in the butt rings to maintain a good tension at all times. Like all rigs that involve tight line off the bottom, it carries the risk of alarming fish and encouraging line bites. At a water like Cassien, however, that is by far the lesser of two evils. Standard ledgering tactics at that carp angler's Mecca will result in countless leads and fish lost in snags.

End result – large carp on the bank.

TACKLE AND TECHNIQUES ─────────

One of the simplest methods of presenting a surface bait, and yet one of the most devastatingly effective, is margin fishing. As its name suggests, this involves fishing in the lake margins, with a bait literally only inches from the bank.

Positioning and Method

The most effective area to choose for such an approach is where there is reasonably deep water adjacent to the bank, where margin patrolling carp can cruise with confidence. It is a method of fishing that obviously demands peace and quiet on the bank, and is unlikely to be successful on a very busy water where there are people, both anglers and non-anglers alike, continually tramping backwards and forwards. For this reason, margin fishing nowadays is only a viable proposition on the more popular waters after dark.

Even at night though, the method demands an abundance of self-control if the fish are not to be alarmed. Conversation must be in whispers and kept to a minimum; nor is impatient shuffling of feet conducive to success. The ability to sit quietly and inconspicuously for long periods is vital for success with this particular method of carp fishing.

Margin fishing gives an angler many advantages over the other methods of surface fishing. Firstly, because you are fishing directly under the rod point, there is no line in the water to alarm the fish, and you can therefore use tackle as strong as you like without any detriment to bait presentation. In fact, as the fishing is at such short range, it is a good idea to step the tackle up a little from the usual strength. A fierce bite and a responding firm strike on a very short line means that there is little natural line stretch to act as a shock absorber. This can cause problems with breakages if you are not careful.

My favourite area for margin fishing, other than the marginal deep water already mentioned, is where such an area is overhung with foliage. Carp love to browse right alongside the bank under the security of the cover provided by the vegetation. The ideal set up is one where the rod is arranged so that the tip only just protrudes from the foliage. Support it with two rests, and when introducing a bait simply wind the bait up to the tip ring well back

Margin Fishing

from the water's edge, quietly and slowly position the rod on the rests and then lower the bait gently until it just rests on the water. Carp that are only feet away from you will not be alarmed if you introduce the bait in such a circumspect manner. It stands to reason that you should set up your camp well away from the water's edge and refrain from showing lights.

Margin fishing is a wonderfully exciting method of fishing but one that is sadly neglected these days. On many waters, as already has been said, there is simply too much bankside disturbance. Where it is possible, however, give it a try. It is great fun, but you must be quiet!

Margin fishing is very exciting.

Tackle and Techniques ———————————

True winter carp fishing begins when the first few cold nights have sent the water temperatures down dramatically. It is not uncommon to see the temperature tumble by as much as 10°F after a couple of night frosts.

The initial temperature drop has a temporarily detrimental effect on most fish, including carp, but when they begin to acclimatize to the changing conditions, they soon begin to feed again. The difference is that, because of a lower metabolic rate, they will feed less often and take less food than they do in the summer. Carp anglers who fish in the winter more than I do say that it is normal for winter fish to feed for two short spells during any 24-hour period. During each of those spells, the timing of which has to be found by trial and error, several fish can be taken in quick succession.

As with barbel fishing, there is evidence that suggests that the going gets progressively tougher as the temperature drops below about 40°F.

Baits

Baits for winter carping are bottom baits in the main, and one which has achieved considerable success is that old faithful luncheon meat. It is often a better winter bait than it is in summer. Particle baits are often a waste of time, a notable exception being sweetcorn, which of course is blessed with a very strong natural smell. Boilies are probably the best bet for winter fishing, and sweeter, more strongly flavoured baits appear to be more successful. If you make your own boilies, try increasing the flavour and sweetener contents for winter fishing.

Perhaps the easiest mistake to make in winter is overuse of free offerings. You are fishing for carp that are only going to be interested in eating a small number of baits, unless the water temperature has suddenly risen dramatically. A large carpet of loose boilies is likely to be counter-productive, and cut down the odds of the hookbait being taken. Winter fishing is the time when the use of PVA stringers really comes into its own. Presenting a small cluster of a few baits around the hook offering is the productive way to fish at this time of the year.

Lastly of course, make sure that you dress for the occasion.

58

Carp Fishing in Winter

Big carp in the snow.

Winter carping is a very static affair, with only an occasional burst of activity, and if you are freezing cold it ceases to be enjoyable but instead becomes downright misery.

59

Baits

Natural food items such as worms, slugs, caterpillars and so on are largely neglected by the majority of modern carp anglers, but they still have their place. Generally speaking, these baits are more effective on waters which have not been totally saturated with boilies. I normally reserve the use of natural baits for those small secluded waters which see little angling pressure, unfortunately becoming rarer these days.

Bloodworms and Lobworms

When carp are engaged in one of their favourite pastimes of browsing over bloodworm beds, one bait that is as likely to yield a bite as any is a redworm or bunch of redworms. Bloodworm feeders usually betray their prescence either by bubbling or disturbing clouds of silt, and perhaps the best approach for those fish is a natural bait. Full-sized lobworms are also good for bubblers, lobs being an excellent carp bait generally. Their only drawback for more extensive use is that they are not selective and can be taken by all other species just as easily. I will therefore only use lobs, apart from when fishing for bubblers or mud stirrers, when stalking a visible individual carp. One very effective ploy when using lobworms is to air-inject the tail with a syringe. Not only does this help to counterbalance the big hook necessary but it ensures that the lob tail wavers clear of the lake bed very enticingly. Needless to say, when using a syringe for angling, take great care that you do not inject yourself with it. Always keep the needle in its guard when not in use.

Such things as caterpillars, slugs of various sizes, leeches, tadpoles and all manner of insects are taken avidly by carp. Obviously, many of them are impossible to use on a hook, but slugs are one of the notable exceptions. They are an excellent stalking bait and, as with chub, carp take them very viciously at times.

In the summer months, carp, like most other fish, will take spent moths and butterflies from the surface, and I know of several carp that have been taken on margin-fished large cabbage white butterflies.

The best known natural bait is of course maggots, and there is no doubt that this is one of the best carp baits of all. Even in a

Natural Baits

water where boilies are used extensively, a local concentration of maggots or casters can often be a very effective ploy. There will be more to say on the use of maggots in the section on particle baits.

Carp love maggots.

BAITS

Apart from natural baits such as lobs and maggots, I would cate-
gorize standard carp baits as those based on plain bread or item
that can be used straight from a tin, such as luncheon meat o
bacon grill.

Bread

For a great many years, most carp caught in this country were
taken on bread in one form or another, and it is still an excellen
and very underrated bait. Floating breadcrust, using a large cube
cut from a tin loaf a few days old, has caught thousands of carp
as has crust ledgered a few inches off the bottom.

For bottom fishing, a ball of plain bread paste will still take its
share of fish, and for fishing over softer bottoms balanced crus

Flake will still take its share of
carp.

62

akes some beating. In this method, the hook is baited with crust and then soft bread paste added until the combined bait just sinks. This ensures that it alights very gently. Also, as the crust section fishes uppermost, the carp initially feels no line.

When you wish to present a slowly sinking bait on the top of very soft bottom weed, there is nothing that fits the bill quite as well as a piece of fresh breadflake, squeezed nearly flat on the hook so that it presents a large surface area when sinking. One of the things that is virtually impossible to reproduce with modern carp baits is the unique texture of breadflake.

All the bread permutations can obviously be varied by doctoring them with any of the flavours, oils or enhancers available nowadays. Balanced crust can be adapted to use any paste you like in place of bread paste. The possibilities are endless.

Tinned Meat

Luncheon meat and bacon grill are now so widely used that they can be classed as standard baits. An effective technique when using these is to bait with a large cube and fish it over a bed of particles. Luncheon meat over a bed of hemp is a deadly method for barbel; it is similarly effective for carp fishing.

A variation when using tinned meats is to use cubes that have been fried for a few minutes, perhaps in the fat you used for breakfast! The fat appears to increase the attraction of the bait. If sufficient frying time is allowed, some of the cubes of meat will be transformed into floaters, and then you can try ledgering off the bottom. Pop-up baits were in use long before boilies were invented! Obviously, a cube of this treated meat can also be used as a true floater. This is useful to know when the attentions of water birds or seagulls make the use of floating crust a frustrating business. They will still find the bait eventually, but it is not so glaringly obvious as bread.

BAITS

The next step up the ladder from standard carp baits are those pastes that have become known as specials. Among the oldest special paste baits are sausage-meat paste and cheese paste which have been around for decades. Both of these are undoubtedly superb baits. Sausage paste is best made by purchasing unskinned meat from a butcher and then mixing it in the proportion of about three to one with the chosen binding agent. This would normally be fine breadcrumbs, but any proprietary ground bait, flour, biscuit meal or even ground up dog biscuits could be used in place of bread. To make an extra spicy sausage paste, try adding a small amount of curry powder. Soft luncheon meat and bacon grill pastes can be produced in exactly the same way.

Cheese and Meat Pastes

Cheese pastes are commonly made by adding grated cheese to plain bread paste. The cheese to use is one that has a strong aroma and my particular favourite is Danish blue. If you prefer a paste with a higher colour, a 50/50 mix of Danish blue and red Leicester gives an attractive bait. For cheese pastes, although there is nothing wrong with using breadcrumbs, I believe a better, softer and more consistent bait is achieved by mixing the grated cheese with soft pastry mix. The result is a wonderfully smooth and pleasant bait to use, and one that stays on the hook well. I would advise against the use of cream cheese in soft pastes, especially if you do much winter carping. The high fat content tends to make the baits harden considerably in cold water. The same comment applies to meat-based pastes, and if it is a soft paste you are aiming at, the leaner the meat you use the less the hardening effect will be. A soft winter sausage paste would therefore be better made from beef sausage-meat rather than from pork, which is much fattier.

More recent years have seen the introduction of such baits as pastes made from stiffening moist pet foods with a binding agent such as breadcrumbs, flour or other dry meals of various kinds. Various commercial cat and dog foods bound with very fine breadcrumbs caught an enormous number of carp in the sixties and early seventies. There is obviously an unlimited permutation of possible mixes by working along these lines.

Special Paste Baits 1

Mixing Paste Baits

The simple definition of a special paste bait is one that is produced by mixing two or more ingredients together to form a consistency that is usable on a hook. Sausage-meat, on its own, is far too soft and tacky to be viable as a hookbait, but mixing it into a stiffish paste with fine crumb or groundbait makes the essential difference. With special pastes, you can give free rein to your imagination. You could choose tinned tuna bound with finely ground breakfast cereals if that took your fancy.

Ingredients such as tinned pet foods, tinned fish, sausage-meat and so on are naturally glutinous, or sticky, and simply require a bulk binding agent to produce a workable bait. However, you may wish to produce a special bait based on a particular dry ingredient. Examples could be salmon or trout fry crumb, almond flour, custard or blancmange powder and so on. In these cases, the ingredients to be added to the chosen powder must include a glutinous content to bind everything together. The simplest material to use is gluten itself, with sufficient water to form a stiff paste. When using gluten, it is important to be careful with the quantity used, since too much will make a bait very rubbery. I always experiment with a new bait, using very small quantities first. Making a note of percentages of each ingredient will then allow a larger batch to be produced once I have the mix to my satisfaction.

Even with very accurate quality control of the amount of gluten used, many baits using gluten and water alone are still quite 'chewy' and a more appealing paste can be produced by adding baby milk powder as well as gluten. Again, the quantity has to be found by trial and error, but the result is a bait that, although still very workable, is less like gum. One of my favourite pastes, and one that has caught me a lot of fish over the years, is trout fry crumb mixed with gluten, baby milk and eggs. The paste can be made with water, but using eggs instead gives the bait a lovely exterior waxy feel. A large ball of paste that has been mixed with eggs can be made very smooth by moulding in the fingers and is therefore more resistant to small fish than the equivalent paste mixed with water.

BAITS

The carp supermarket.

Paste Bait Content

The special paste baits mentioned in this section are what I call natural, in that they are produced entirely from ingredients available at any grocery store or pet shop. To recap, these could include tinned meats, tinned fish, moist and dried pet foods, biscuits, flours of all kinds, dessert powders such as custard or blancmange, savoury powders such as curry, cheeses, sausage rusk, baby milk powders and breakfast cereals. You can doubtless add dozens of examples of your own. Pastes made from all of these bases tend to have low- to medium-protein content and when you are looking to make high-protein paste baits, we are

66

Special Paste Baits 2

moving towards more what I call synthetic special pastes. By this I mean baits that are produced from the more specialized materials available from tackle dealers. Using these, you are more able to control the final protein content of your finished bait. The general principle behind producing a good synthetic special is to keep a balance between lighter ingredients and those that are much more dense and bulky. A theoretical mixture with a very high protein content may turn out to be totally useless and unworkable as a practical bait so, as with the natural specials, some considerable experimentation is called for. Keep a careful note of your experiments, so that you will be able to repeat them when you have established a few good recipes.

The last point to make about natural special pastes is that they can all be covered in a skin by boiling if eggs have been used in their preparation. If you have a paste that is taking a few nice fish, say ground almonds, gluten and baby milk powder bound with eggs, you may wish to continue using the mixture even though the attentions of smaller fish are proving troublesome. The way to do this is to roll the paste into balls and drop them into boiling water for a couple of minutes. The resulting rubbery skin acts as a deterrent to the bait being taken by small fish. This process was the origin of the first crude boilies.

BAITS

On most carp waters today, boilies of one kind or another hav
become the standard bait, and there is no doubt at all that the
have revolutionized carp angling. If you are a carp-only angle
you may elect to make your own baits so that you can be sure c
presenting something to the fish that is totally unique to yoursel
However, there is now less need to go to the trouble of hom
preparation as the present range of commercially available boilie
is mind boggling. The quality of the baits has improved immea
sureably over the last few years and many of our top carp angler
no longer make their own mixes, catching plenty of carp on th
bait dealers have to offer.

Varieties of Commercial Boilies

Basically, there are two distinct types of commercially availabl
boilies, either frozen or shelf life. My personal preference is fc
frozen baits, although I will readily accept that for the long-sta
angler, or the angler that regularly spends a week or so fishing o
the Continent, frozen baits are inconvenient. For any session th;
is likely to extend to more than three days, shelf-life baits are th
answer, unless you have access to freezing facilities. One thing t

Commercial boilies.

Commercial Boiled Baits

be wary of, however, is that your shelf-life bait packets do not become torn. The slightest pinhole-sized puncture will allow ingress of enough air for the baits to spoil and go mouldy in a very short time.

Obviously, it is up to the individual which particular brand of boilies he or she uses, but I have no hesitation whatever in recommending the Richworth range from Streamselect Ltd. They have always been of superb quality and are proven fish catchers, both frozen and shelf life being available. I have now lost count of the good fish I have caught on them, and in tutti frutti, Richworth must have the most successful carp bait ever produced.

One alternative from Richworth, which overcomes the objection of a bait not being unique to the angler, is their neutral boilies, which anglers flavour and enhance with their own additives. This is achieved by a process of atomization, where the chosen flavours are added to the frozen boilies in a resealable bag and then left to thaw. The thawing process sees the baits draw the flavour in .by capillary action until they become thoroughly impregnated.

Sizes

Several different sizes of boilies are available, from pea-sized mini-boilies right up to those with an 18mm diameter. The largest size is useful for very big carp, and mini-boilies have proved their worth as a bed of prebait over which more normal sized boilies are offered on the terminal rig. Floating boilies are also available commercially in some types of shelf-life baits, and these are useful if you do not want to go to the trouble of preparing your own floaters for pop-up rigs.

Baits

If you decide to make your own boiled baits at home, either because you want to produce a unique bait, a non-standard size or shape, or simply because you enjoy it, there are several ways you can go about it. For example, you may require a proven fish catching bait in a very large size if you fish a water with a large head of tench, as these can take the largest commercially available boilie quite easily. If this is the case, a ready-mixed bait like Rod Hutchinson's Black Juice could be used, where you prepare the boilies to whatever size you require.

If you want to prepare a bait with your own secret blend of flavours, sweeteners, enhancers and oils, or try the same bait in a variety of colours, then you may wish to use a ready-prepared base mix to which you add your chosen additives and eggs. There are some very good base mixes on the market, in a variety of protein contents and which do different jobs. There are mixes based on birdseed, groundnut blends, milk product blends and so on. There are so many that it is very easy to confuse yourself and I would generally recommend sticking to one mix you are happy with. The Richworth 50/50 base mix is as good as any.

Many people enjoy making their own baits from basic principles, developing their own base mixes to achieve specific results. A base mix must have the ability to be made into a usable bait that will not fall apart after ten minutes in the water, and some theoretical mixes will not be possible in practice. As I have said before, it is a good general principle to have a rough balance between light constituents and those that are much denser.

Ingredients

A list of well-proven carp bait ingredients would include edible casein, sodium and calcium caseinates, wheat gluten and wheat flour, soya flour and soya isolate, lactalbumin, groundnuts of various types, cornflour, maize meal, rice flour, oatmeal, ground bird foods, fish meals of various kinds, and various branded mineral or protein supplements such as Codlivine, Equivite, Yestamin or PYM.

To avoid undue confusion, it is best to utilize only a few of these ingredients in each of your base mixes, and two examples from my own fishing are:

70

Home-Made Boilies

50 per cent edible casein	25 per cent edible casein
20 per cent soya flour	25 per cent sodium caseinate
10 per cent wheat gluten	10 per cent wheat gluten
10 per cent lactalbumin	10 per cent lactalbumin
10 per cent Equivite	10 per cent wheat germ
	20 per cent Ostermilk

You can then add whatever you like to produce the finished bait. It could be naturally flavoured ingredients such as fish meals or peanut meal, or it could be a sweeter flavour such as custard powder. Alternatively, the whole range of concentrated essences is at your disposal.

Protein Content

The protein content of the finished bait is determined by the base mix. As a general rule of thumb, the milk products such as casein, the caseinates and lactalbumin are high in protein, as are glutens, while most cereal flours such as rice, corn, wheat or oats are of low protein. The same applies to flours of nuts such as peanuts and walnuts. Soya flour and isolate has about a medium level, as has wheat germ. As might be expected, meals of fish such as herring or mackerel or any lean meats are high in protein.

From the above, it can be seen that it is possible largely to control the protein content of a base mix by selecting carefully from the range of ingredients available. The overriding factor will always be, though, that the quantities of the ingredients selected are compatible in producing a mix that is of practical use in making a bait that will hold together.

Ingredients for home-made boilies.

71

BAITS

Having weighed and measured all the ingredients for your bait, it is now time to start preparing your boilies. As a general rule, a total 1lb of ingredients will enable about 200 14mm baits to be made.

Making Boilies

First, thoroughly mix all the dry ingredients together, making sure that there are no lumps. I go to the trouble of sieving all the ingredients first. The dry mix is then added slowly to the well-beaten eggs and thoroughly mixed with a wooden spoon to form an even, stiff paste. Any additional liquid ingredients such as flavours, enhancers or colourings should be mixed with the eggs before the paste is made. The composition of your mix will determine exactly how many eggs will be required to form a paste of the correct consistency, but four large eggs will be about right for 1lb of dry material.

When the paste is of uniform consistency, break it down into conveniently sized lumps and roll each into sausage like strips of

Equipment for making your
own boiled baits.

72

Home-Made Boilies and Floater

the diameter you require for the finished baits. Next, chop the sausages into segments, $^5/_8$in is about right for a standard-sized bait, and roll them into balls between the palms of your hands. Alternatively, of course, you can equip yourself with one of those commercially available boilie rolling machines, which make this tedious part of the job so much quicker.

The next job is to skin the baits by boiling. To do this drop a few of the baits at a time into boiling water, and leave them there for your selected time. The longer they are boiled the harder they will become. I generally boil mine for about a minute. You need to be sure that all the baits receive a similar boiling time, and to do that I suggest you use an old chip pan or something similar for ease of lifting the baits all at once in and out of the boiling water pan.

It is important not to touch the baits too much while they are still hot or you will distort their shape. Obviously, perfectly round baits are preferable for long-distance fishing because of their aero-dynamic properties. The hot baits should therefore be tipped on to a clean tea towel and left alone until they are perfectly cold. At that stage, they can be bagged either for fishing the next day, or for the freezer if you are making a large supply.

Making Floaters

For producing floaters, most boilie mixes can be made to float by the simple expedient of doubling up the number of eggs in the mixture. This will transform the stiff paste into a much runnier mixture, which can then be baked inside a hot oven in exactly the same way as making a cake. I usually use a fairly shallow old cake tin for the purpose, and it is a good idea to grease the tin very lightly before introducing the mixture, to avoid sticking. Different boilie mixes will be found to give different consistencies of floater and it is a matter of trial and error. You can achieve either a very heavy, dense floating bait or one that is extremely light, open and crusty, or any combination in between.

BAITS

Flavours

You only have to look along the shelves of modern tackle shops to see just how extensive the range of flavours available to carp anglers is today. There are literally hundreds of alternatives you can choose from, and it is very easy to become totally confused. Do not fall into the very common trap of buying bottles of many varied flavours and trying batches of different flavoured baits every time you go fishing. You will learn very little from that kind of haphazard approach. The best way is to select two flavour alternatives that you initially intend to concentrate on, and give them a fair trial. I generally start a new season with one flavour only, and gradually introduce a second when results start to tail off, if they do.

Most of the commercially available flavours are in highly concentrated form and you should be sparing in the quantity you use in your bait mix. Most manufacturers advise on the correct dosage, and I would say that you rarely need more than 5ml/lb of bait. Too much flavour can act as a repellent rather than attractant, by making the baits bitter. Remember also, that carp have a much more sensitive olfactory system than ours. A dose that we cannot smell will be very obvious to the fish.

With such a wide choice of excellent flavours, it is impossible to give advice about which you should use. However, I can say with absolute certainty that the following list of flavours and flavour mixtures has caught me a tremendous number of carp. They are: maple cream; maple; maple/butter; strawberry; butter; strawberry/butter; strawberry/cream; butter/cream; scopex; butter/toffee; scopex/strawberry; blue cheese; peanut; hazelnut; almond; almond/toffee; caramel/cream; cinnamon; peach; peach/cream; golden syrup; and ultra spice.

Colours

Much of the time, colouring baits is an angler's whim and is used simply as a convenient method of identifying batches of different flavoured baits. However, on occasions I have found that brightly coloured baits outfished duller ones, and I generally opt for bright red, orange or yellow. These obviously show up like beacons on

Flavours and Colours

dark lake beds so, conversely, it would be worth trying black, brown, dark blue or green baits over a very light sandy bottom.

You will only get visual advantage from brightly coloured baits in fairly shallow water, say up to about 6ft in depth. At much greater depth than that, all baits will appear the same. I once carried out an experiment at a shallow water of an average depth of little more than 3ft, and the carp showed a definite preference for orange baits over my green alternative of the same mix. The same experiment in a much deeper water showed an equal number of fish to each version.

There are hundreds of flavours available.

75

BAITS

As well as naturally flavoured ingredients and synthetic concentrated flavours, there are also sweeteners, flavour enhancers, appetite stimulators and oils that can be added to carp baits to increase their attractiveness and pulling power. There are a vast array of additives on the market that would come into the above categories, from many different manufacturers and with many different exotic names, and it can all become very confusing. As with the choice of flavours, I would strongly recommend confining

Sweeteners, enhancers and oils.

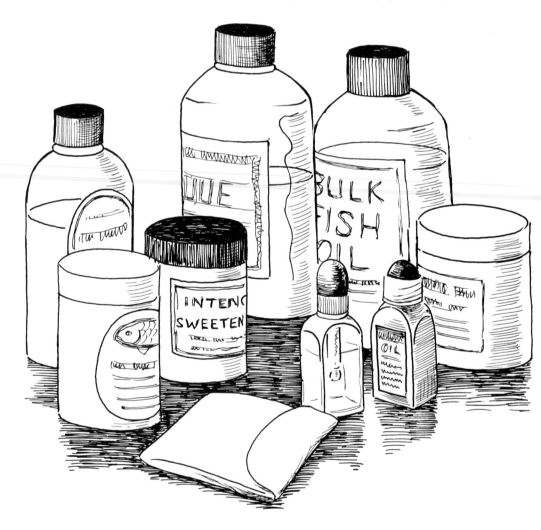

Sweetners, Flavour Enhancers and Oils

your attentions to one or two additives for a particular bait and sticking with them long enough for meaningful conclusions to be drawn.

Sweetners and Flavour Enhancers

I generally adopt the rule of thumb that I add concentrated sweetner and appetite stimulator to naturally sweeter flavours such as strawberry, cinnamon or scopex, but with the more savoury flavours such as cheese, ultra spice or any meat or fish, I substitute the sweetner for flavour enhancer and use that in conjunction with the appetite stimulator. Perhaps my most successful home-made bait of all was Richworth 50/50 base mix flavoured with peanut and sweetened with concentrated sweetner. Dosage was 10ml of flavour per 1lb of bait and 5ml of sweetner. I do not normally recommend such a high level of flavour and sweetner as that, but that bait was dynamite and caught carp everywhere I went.

Oils

The newest innovation in the carp bait scene is the use of essential oils, together with a whole range of new additives that go with them, and this can become a very complex subject indeed. It is one of which I have limited first-hand experience at present and I can do no better than recommend the reader to study the literature put out by the people in the know, such as Rod Hutchinson, Bob Baker of Streamselect Ltd, and Tim Paisley of Nutrabaits. Rod Hutchinson's small book on baits, available from any good tackle shop, is a particularly useful guide to modern carp bait additives, and is essential reading if you really want to come to grips with what is undoubtedly a fascinating subject.

BAITS _____

The theory that fish are preoccupied with large quantities of small food items is one that has been proved many times and occurs naturally in nature. You have only to see how totally absorbed a carp becomes when feeding on bloodworm colonies – it will usually ignore everything else.

There are very often times when carp will not be responsive to large selective baits such as boilies and on these occasions the answer is to fish for them with particle baits. But to be successful, you have to attain preoccupied feeding on the baits, so this means having a sufficient concentration of particles in a small area, so that they actually outnumber the individual items of natural food that are available. Unless you are fishing an exceptionally small water, it is totally impossible to preoccupy the entire carp stock with your chosen particle, as you would have to buy bait by the lorry load!

Prebaiting

The technique is therefore to heavily bait selected small areas and then make sure that your casting is very accurate. It may sound very obvious for me to say that it is a grave mistake to prebait one area and then introduce your hookbait in another, but it is amazing how often I see it in practice. You must have your hookbait among your free offerings to stand any reasonable chance of success. Remember, you are not relying on the individual attraction of your hookbait, such as with a large boilie. It is the carpet of many hundreds of baits that is the attraction.

I would define particle baits as those that are big enough to be used on their own, or with two or three others, on a big hook, and the best known are sweetcorn, chick peas, maple peas, black-eyed beans, peanuts, tiger nuts and sultanas. Commercially available mini-boilies would also come in this category.

Method

Before using any particle bait, make sure that any dried seeds, peas, nuts or beans are well soaked before use, so that any swelling that takes place has occurred before entering the carp's

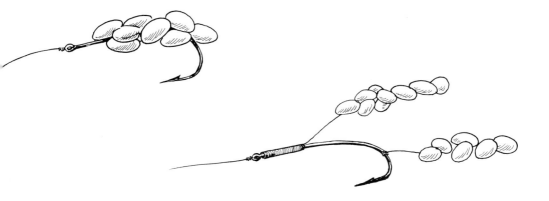

Particle presentation variations.

gut, otherwise it could cause distress or even death. Particle baits must be used responsibly. To be doubly sure that your baits are safe to use, it is often best to boil them for a few minutes to ensure that they cannot germinate. Obviously, this is only necessary with beans and seeds that are naturally sprouting. However, some very hard baits like tiger nuts are best pressure cooked to ensure that they are soft enough to be easily broken down by the fish. With normal beans and seeds it is only necessary to boil them for a few minutes after presoaking. You only want to prevent germination; overboiling will destroy their attractiveness.

A good ploy is to keep beans and seeds in the water in which they were boiled. In fact, results have shown that the baits can become better fish catchers if they have been kept under their liquid for a few days. They become much stronger smelling, which the carp appear to find more appealing. Obviously, bait that has begun to smell sour should not be used.

If you want to offer the carp a particle bait that is a little different, you can flavour and colour particles as you do boilies. Seeds, beans and nuts can be soaked and boiled in water to which has been added any flavour of your choice. However, as many synthetic flavours evaporate during boiling, it is best to stick to natural flavours and syrups. Any soup can be used, as can molasses, curry sauce or maple syrup. Again, you can give free rein to your imagination.

For loose feeding with particles, a catapult is obviously adequate for close-range work, with a wide pouch enabling a

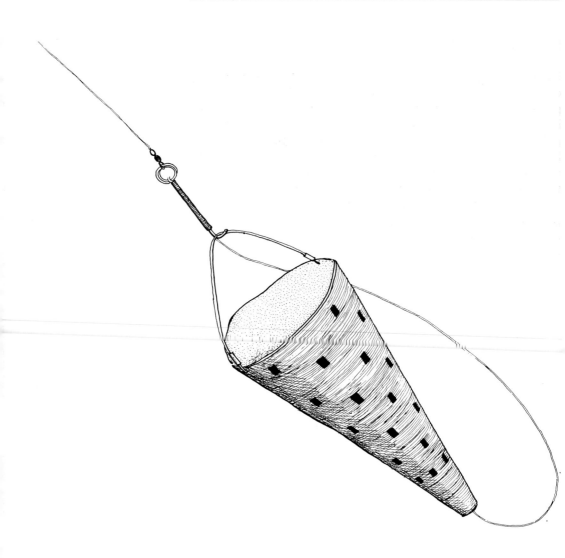

'Whopper-dropper' particle.

good handful of bait to be introduced each time. However, where you wish to bait at longer range than is possible with a catapult, I would recommend one of those special particle bait droppers, commercially called bait rockets. They make long-range baiting with particles very easy and very accurate, but you need a powerful rod to cast them. I always take an old 3lb test curve pike rod to cast my bait rocket.

80

Particle Baits 2

Floating Particles

Particle bait fishing is not confined to bottom baits. Presenting drifting multiple baits is a very effective way of taking carp. Some particle baits will be naturally buoyant, and these would include breakfast cereals such as puffed wheat and sugar puffs, trout pellets or floating pellets sold for use by koi keepers, dog and cat biscuits or synthetic floater cake cut into very small cubes and used as a multiple bait. Most of these will be too light to support the weight of a carp hook and so are best fished in conjunction with a hook that has been counterbalanced with rig foam or polystyrene. I like to use two or three floating particles on the terminal rig, and drift them down the wind among two or three pouchfuls of free offerings.

BAITS _____

Preoccupied feeding in carp depends on a large quantity of individual bait items being present, and it therefore follows that the smaller each item is the more of them there will be to the pound and the more preoccupied feeding will be likely. A quantity of 5lb of hempseed is therefore more likely to achieve the desired effect than is 5lb of sweetcorn, which in turn will contain more individual particles than 5lb of tiger nuts. We can therefore see that we take the theory of particle fishing to its ultimate conclusion by baiting with very small particles, which are termed mass baits. My definition of a mass bait is one that is impossible to use individually on a large carp hook, and the most obvious example and perhaps the best, is hempseed. Others are dari seeds, boiled rice, pearl barley, stewed wheat and tares. Wheat and tares are about as large as I go in defining a true mass bait.

We have two main hookbait alternatives when fishing over beds of mass baits, either using a cluster of the bait itself or fishing one individual larger item. For fishing clusters, of hemp for example, twenty or so seeds can be superglued to a large hook in a caddis case kind of arrangement and arranged to lie in wait amongst the free offerings. Alternatively, you can still utilize a hair rig by glueing smaller clusters of seeds on a hair or multiple hairs. Or you can glue strings of individual seeds along multiple hairs.

Varieties

Perhaps the most effective use of mass baits is as a background attraction over which you fish a much larger hookbait, and in fact this is one of the most deadly presentations. I have taken many carp fishing in this manner, and examples from my diaries are fish taken by presenting bacon grill over hemp, boilies and pop-up boilies over hemp, peanuts, tiger nuts or rice, lobworms over hemp and luncheon meat over wheat.

The best known mass baits of the lot are obviously maggots and casters, which carp love as do most species of fish. Their problem is the expense of using them in quantity. A good ploy when using maggots is to fish a large writhing bunch of them, perhaps twenty on a big hook, in the midst of the bait carpet. To give a very effective mass bait effect with maggots, another excellent method is to fish a bunch of large maggots over a bed of squatts. Squatts

Mass Baits

are good as they die quickly under water and are therefore much less likely to crawl away from where they are introduced. As I said, though, money has to be no object to achieve preoccupation with maggots, as gallons have to be used to attain anything but a very temporary effect. This is even more true with casters, which are dearer still.

Preoccupied feeding.

For anything but short-range fishing, one of the difficulties is ensuring that the hookbait is being fished in the proximity of the free offerings or loose feed. The longer the range you wish to place your baits, the more acute this problem becomes. The angler seeking roach or bream has recourse to the swimfeeder to concentrate feed around his hookbait, but of course this is not feasible for the carp angler using boilies. It is certainly advantageous if a hookbait can be presented as part of a little cluster of baits, as the cluster itself will have enhanced attraction for the carp.

Science has come to the carp angler's aid in solving this problem with a remarkable material called polyvinyl alcohol, or PVA for short, which is a tough, plastic film-like material when dry, but rapidly dissolves when coming into contact with moisture. Most good tackle shops sell PVA as either string, bags or

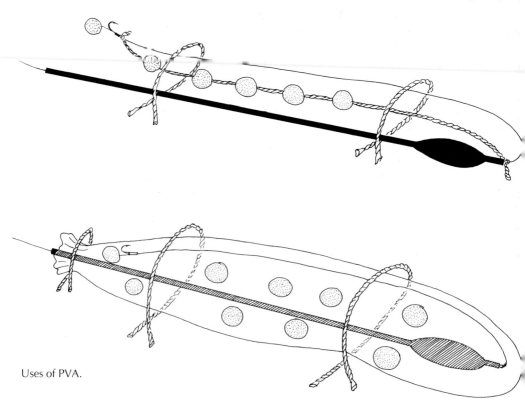

Uses of PVA.

tubes. The rate of dissolution of the material depends on its thickness, but string the diameter of 12lb monofilament will dissolve in cold water in a matter of seconds.

Method

String is the most popular variety of PVA, and we use it to make what are termed stringers. Several boilies are threaded on a length of PVA with a baiting needle and then tied along the terminal rig hook length as shown in the diagram. If you are not proposing to cast very far, one end of the stringer can simply be tied to the hook bend and the whole lot cast out as it is. However, that gives a large amount of air resistance on the cast, and it is far more aerodynamic if the stringer is tied back tightly along the terminal tackle.

As well as string, PVA casting tubes also have their uses, but it must be stressed that these offer even more air resistance than stringers. You cannot fish at long range with tubes, but where they do come in useful is in presenting a large cluster of particles right around the hookbait. It goes without saying that the particles should be bone-dry before use, otherwise you will end up with a gooey mess. I spread particles on a towel to dry if I intend introducing a PVA tube with each recast.

One last use for PVA string is in preventing tangling on the cast. I have already mentioned ways of preventing soft hook link materials from tangling, by using either anti-tangle tubing or stiffening gel, but if we assume that you have neither to hand, a simple way of overcoming the problem is to tie the hook link back up the main line with a tie of PVA string. As well as making tangling on the cast impossible, it also maximizes your casting range by minimizing the wind resistance of the terminal rig.

85

BAITS

Prebaiting with boilies.

By prebaiting, I mean introducing free offerings not just at the start of a session, but days or even weeks in advance of commencing fishing. On a little-fished water, especially if there is a fairly small head of carp that are well scattered and you do not have too much competition from other anglers, then prebaiting is definitely advantageous. If it is carried out sensibly and to a predetermined plan then it can concentrate the fish into your designated area and greatly increase your chances of success.

Method

The principle behind prebaiting is obviously to get the carp feeding confidently on the selected bait in the area where you intend to fish for them. Say I was prebaiting a fairly small water with a small head of carp for several weeks with boilies. To start with, I would introduce bait all over the lake, with no particular emphasis on one swim. This is to get the carp used to finding the bait and, hopefully, liking it enough to search for more. Gradually, the baiting would be tightened so that the bulk of the free offerings were in or around the selected fishing area, and over the last few days before fishing only the swim itself would be baited. I would be trying to create a preferred feeding site for the fish.

Drawbacks

The above method of concentrating carp in an area has been proved effective many times, but it has serious drawbacks. Firstly, for it to work, the period of prebaiting has to be extensive, sometimes over several weeks. The baiting sessions have to be regular, at least every other day, and it goes without saying that this involves a lot of time, effort and, not least important, money. It is no good attempting such a campaign with, say fifty boilies every other day. For the technique to work, you must use large quantities of bait and that is expensive. If you cannot afford to do the job properly then it is a waste of time and petrol trying, as you will achieve nothing. The bait must be introduced in sufficient quantity for it to become a major part of the carp's diet.

Prebaiting

On most of our better known carp waters, prebaiting is no longer advisable, for two reasons. Firstly, you can never be absolutely sure that you will be able to get the swim you want on the day of fishing, and there is nothing more galling than to see another angler catching fish over your loose feed. Secondly, carp in the popular waters see boilies of all different flavours in all parts of the lake anyway, and your prebaits will seem little different to the fish. On a popular water, then, you could go to a lot of time, trouble and expense and achieve nothing more than you could achieve without any prebaiting whatever, other than introducing free offerings on the actual fishing session itself.

Get the carp used to finding the bait.

Heavily Fished Waters

There is one circumstance on a heavily fished water where prebaiting can be very effective, but it would still depend on being able to get the swim on the day of fishing. A water that is constantly being hammered on boilies can respond very well to localized concentrations of particles and if you are able to build up a hot spot of, say hempseed or wheat, you could catch quite a few bonus carp in quick succession.

CARP CARE _____

I see more carp lost on the strike than at any time, and the reason is one of poor striking technique. It is very easy, after perhaps hours or days of inactivity, to thrash the rod wildly in excitement as line starts to disappear off the spool. As often as not, this leads to striking on a partially slack line, which results either in the carp being missed completely or such an insecure hookhold being established that the hook pulls out after a few seconds.

Striking

Upon having a run, the first essential is to keep calm. Pick up the rod, close the bale arm if you are fishing an open-spool technique and then wait a second or two for the line to tighten properly. Only when you see the line becoming taut should you strike, firmly but smoothly. Do not make a sudden, vicious snatch of a strike or that could lead to an overload on the tackle and break the line.

Playing a Fish

Provided that your hook is as sharp as it should be, striking in that fashion should see a solid hookhold and you may then find yourself locked in battle with one of the most powerful fish that swims in British fresh water. There are two schools of thought as to the correct technique for actual playing of the fish: many anglers swearing by fighting the fish off a properly set slipping clutch, while others advocating backwinding. Personally, I prefer playing big fish on strong tackle by use of the clutch. I believe this method enables me to utilize the power of the tackle at my disposal more effectively. Provided that the rod and line are balanced, the clutch should start to yield when the rod reaches a quarter-circle deflection. This should be preset before fishing and regularly checked during the session. Because of inertia, it takes a greater pull to start the clutch slipping than it does to keep it slipping, so the technique to employ when a carp is taking line against the drag is to apply finger pressure to the rim of the spool. This pressure can be increased whenever the carp heads towards danger areas.

Playing Carp

When the carp is not taking line, you can recover line by a process known as pumping. Wind the rod with the point down towards the fish and then, with finger on the reel spool to prevent it slipping, draw the rod back smoothly over your shoulder. Having completed that manoeuvre, wind down again, taking up the recovered line. Obviously, your finger can be removed from the spool rim at any time if the carp makes another surge.

Increase pressure when carp heads for snags.

Backwind

Backwinding is favoured by many of our leading big fish anglers, and I employ it on occasions myself when using much lighter terminal rigs, where inertia problems with the clutch become more significant. With backwinding, you simply fish with the anti-reverse on the reel in the 'off' position, so that the reel is free to rotate backwards as well as forwards. Quite simply, when you assess that the fish should be given line you wind the reel backwards to suit. The major drawback with the technique in my estimation is that human nature being what it is, you almost invariably give line much earlier than you need.

CARP CARE

Having landed our carp, we have a collective responsibility to ensure that it is returned to the water unharmed and having undergone the minimum stress possible. The first essential is to prevent the fish from doing itself any damage by jumping on a hard bank. For this purpose I would recommend one of the modern unhooking mats, and nowhere is this more true than when fishing gravel pits. Make sure that the mat is good and wet before use, or you will remove much of the carp's protective slime. Even on a soft mat, it is important to prevent the fish from flapping around, and a good ploy is to cover its eyes with a wet carp sack or something similar.

Before carrying out any manoeuvres such as weighing or photographing the fish, always prepare the equipment first, before you even pick up the carp. The less time it is handled, the better. Obviously, weigh-slings should be also thoroughly wetted before use.

Photographing Your Catch

When taking photographs, there is always a danger of a large fish kicking and for this reason do not be tempted to hold the carp too far off the ground. You want to avoid dropping fish at all times, obviously, but if it does happen despite all your precautions, it will do little harm if the fish only drops a few inches onto a soft mat. Also, if you sense a carp starting to squirm and you feel there is imminent danger of your dropping it, cradle the fish gently but

Always use an unhooking mat.

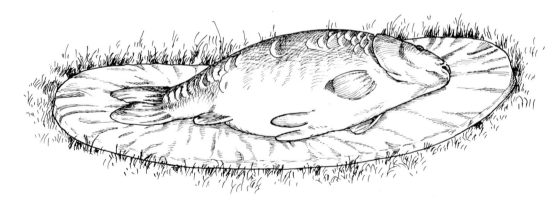

firmly in to your body until its struggles subside. For this reason, it is best to wear either a smooth waterproof coat or soft shirt while being photographed. A very rough garment could remove slime and scales from a carp if you had to clutch it close to stop it wriggling.

Never carry a carp back to the water in your arms; always use the weigh-sling. It is all a matter of common sense really. Nothing is too much trouble to ensure that these beautiful fish are kept in pristine condition.

Use of Carp Sacks

Lastly, if the water you are fishing allows the use of carp sacks for retaining fish for trophy shots, please use them responsibly. There is nothing wrong with this retention method, but please buy top-quality, soft sacks from reputable manufacturers, and ones that have plenty of holes for adequate throughflow of water. Make sure that the sack is positioned in such a way that the carp has plenty of room and the sack material is not drawn tightly round its gills, preventing proper respiration. And please do not leave a carp in a sack in shallow water under a hot sun; it will suffer greatly from the heat and deoxygenation. In all my years of big fish angling, I have never lost a fish in a sack. It is only a matter of taking that little bit of extra care.

Use carp sacks responsibly.

GLOSSARY _____

Anchored baits   Buoyant baits either submerged or floating, held in position by bottom lead.
Anti-tangle gel   Special, water-soluble gel to stiffen limp hook links, preventing tangling on casting.
Anti-tangle rig   Any rig designed to prevent tangling on cast. Usually incorporates stiff plastic tubing.
Atomization   Flavouring frozen boiled baits by spraying and then allowing to thaw in a sealed bag.

Back stop   Swivel or stop knot above the lead, preventing it from sliding too far.
Backwinding   Method of playing fish by fishing with the anti-reverse of fixed spool off, and giving line to a running fish by winding the handle backwards.
Bait dropper   Plastic cage for dropping loose feed into a swim.
Baitrunner   Fixed-spool reel with a facility to allow fish to run line off freely with the anti-reverse on.
Balanced crust   A neutral buoyancy bait, of breadcrust and bread paste.
Beachcaster rig   Special rig for fishing anchored floating bait at range. Only suitable for quite shallow water.
Boilie   Modern carp paste, mixed with eggs, moulded into balls and boiled to give tough skin.
Boilie stop   Small piece of plastic holding boilie on to hair rig loop.
Bolt rig   Terminal rig using heavy lead, designed to make fish bolt on feeling resistance.
Bow waving   Carp swimming close to the surface, such that the dorsal fin forms bow wave.
Bubblers   Carp feeding in silty bottom, sending up clouds of bubbles.
Butt foam   Foam to insert in butt ring, to ensure that line remains tight.

Carp sack   Soft perforated sack for retaining carp for a photograph.

'D' rig   Special hair rig, where bait slides along a D-shaped nylon loop.

Fast taper   A rod designed for long casting, where the taper from butt to tip is much steeper than normal.

Hair rig   Carp rig where bait is mounted on fine line or other material off the hook.
Hair rig needle   Implement for attaching boilie to loop on the end of the hair.
Head and tailing   Carp leaving the water in porpoise-like fashion, head first and then the tail.

Margin fishing   Fishing a floating bait under the rod top.
Mass baits   Very small particle baits, such as hempseed.
Monkey climber   Bite indicator consisting of a plastic tube sliding up and down a metal rod.

Glossary

Particle baits   Small baits used in large quantities, such as peanuts, tiger nuts, maple peas and so on.

Paternoster   Method of fishing whereby the hook link is attached above the lead on the terminal rig.

Pop-up rigs   Bottom fishing with buoyant hookbaits.

Prebaiting   Preparing a swim with feed before fishing.

PVA   Polyvinyl alcohol. Waxy, membrane-like material, extremely rapidly water soluble.

Rig foam   Foam-like material, used for making buoyant baits or terminal rigs.

Rotten bottom   Lead link of low breaking strain line, which breaks easily if it becomes snagged.

Self-cocking float   Float that cocks under its own weight, and does not need additional weight on the terminal rig.

Sliding hair rig   Hair rig free to slide along hook link.

Sliding stop knot   Special knot, for creating adjustable back stops.

Slipping clutch   The gearing on a fixed-spool reel, which allows a fish to take line when the anti-reverse is on.

Smoke screener   A carp swimming through bottom mud or silt, creating a cloud, or smoke screen.

Stalking   Casting to individual carp you can see, usually in margins.

Suspender rig   Rig for fishing floating baits at long range either floating or anchored. Especially useful over water too deep for a beachcaster rig.

USEFUL ADDRESSES ─────────────

Anglers' Cooperative Association, Midland Bank Chambers, Westgate, Grantham, Lincolnshire.
The Carp Society, 33 Covert Road, Hainault, Ilford, Essex.
National Association of Specialist Anglers, Dr K. Fickling, Kilgarth, 27 Lodge Lane, Upton, Gainsborough, Lincolnshire.

There are many Carp Society agencies across the country. A few are listed below:

Addlestone Angling, 166 Station Road, Addlestone, Surrey.
Bob Morris Tackle, 1 Lincolnshire Terrace, Land End, Darenth, Dartford, Kent.
Cotswold Angling, Kennedy's Garden Centre, Hyde Road, Swindon, Wiltshire.
Cuttle Mill Fishery, Cuttle Mill Lane, Wishaw, Warwickshire.
Foster's Tackle, Kings Road, Kingstanding, Birmingham.
Garston Angling, 8 St Mary's Road, Garston, Liverpool.
Harefield Tackle, 9 Park Lane, Harefield, Middlesex.
Leslies of Luton, 74 Park Street, Luton, Bedfordshire.
Nutrabaits, 95 Main Street, North Anston, Sheffield, West Yorkshire.
Simpsons of Turnford, Nunsbury Drive, Turnford, Hertfordshire.
Trafford Angling Supplies, 34 Moss Road, Stretford, Manchester.
Veals Tackle, 61 Old Market, Bristol, Avon.
Walkers of Trowell, Nottingham Road, Trowell, Nottinghamshire.

Further Reading

Bailey, John, *Carp – The Quest for the Queen,* (The Crowood Press, 1984).

Clifford, Kevin, *Master Fisherman – Carp,* (Beekay Publishers, 1990).

Clifford, Kevin and Arbery, Len, *Redmire Pool,* (Beekay Publishers, 1984).

Gibbinson, Jim, *Modern Specimen Hunting,* (Beekay Publishers, 1983).

Gibbinson, Jim, *Big Water Carp,* (Beekay Publishers, 1989).

Hutchinson, Rod, *The Carp Strikes Back,* (Wonderdog Public's, 1983).

Little, Andy, *Guide to Carp Fishing,* (Hamlyn Press, 1988).

Maddocks, Kevin, *Guide to Carp Waters,* (Beekay Publishers, 1986).

Maddocks, Kevin, *Carp Fever,* (Beekay Publishers, tenth edition 1988).

Miles, Tony, *The Complete Specimen Hunter,* (The Crowood Press, 1989).

Paisley, Tim, *Carp Fishing,* (The Crowood Press, 1988).

Turnbull, Chris, *Big Fish from Famous Waters,* (David & Charles, 1990).

Various, *Top Ten,* (Beekay Publishers, 1983).

Wilson, John, *Go Fishing,* (Boxtree Ltd, 1989).

Yates, Chris, *Casting at the Sun,* (Pelham Books, 1986).

INDEX